IGNITE AZUSA

Positioning for a New Jesus Revolution

Jennifer A. Miskov, Ph.D.

with Heidi Baker, Lou Engle, and Bill Johnson

Silver to Gold

Silver to Gold
2391 Placer Street
Redding, CA 96001, USA

ISBN:
978-0-9842370-6-7
0-9842370-6-2

Interior Design by Jonathan McGraw: jonathanmcgraw.net
Graphic Design by David Stoddard: mediarevelation.com

Headshot by Kenny Morgan: kennethmorganphoto.com
Wave photo by Jennifer A. Miskov
Carrie Judd Montgomery photo used with permission by the Christian and Missionary Alliance Archive Center: cmalliance.org
Evan Roberts photo used with permission from Moriah Chapel: moriahchapel.org.uk
All other pre- and Azusa related photographs used with permission by Flower Pentecostal Heritage Center: ifphc.org

Visit the author's website at silvertogold.com

From the moment I opened up *Ignite Azusa* and began reading the preface entitled "The Current of Revival is Sweeping by Our Door," I began to weep! The presence of the Holy Spirit filled my room and I was not able to put the book down until I completed it. Jennifer A. Miskov skillfully crafts together the history and impact of this most significant move of God. But even more than that, *Ignite Azusa* fans the flame of the testimony of contemporary revivalists such as Heidi Baker, Lou Engle, and Bill Johnson, marrying the past to the present and releasing us all into the fullness of the future! This book is a must read for this season and for this generation. There truly is a current of revival that is sweeping by our door. Let's not miss our chance to ride this wave.

SHERI DOWNS
1st Year Revival Group Pastor for
Bethel School of Supernatural Ministry

When I read *Ignite Azusa*, it felt like the Holy Spirit was reading it to me. Every page speaks of deep prophetic significance and implications. My heart is lit on fire all over again, utterly amazed at what God has done in the past, and filled with great expectancy for what He is about to do in our midst. We are on the precipice, a tipping point of another great move of God in America and in the nations of the earth. *Ignite Azusa* has fueled my hunger for revival and to see God move mightily in my generation! Fasten your seat belts; it's going to be a wild ride!

CORNELIUS QUEK
M.Div., Founding Director of 7K and Elisha's Room

There are certain books written on revival that ignite a fire inside, causing my heart to cry out for God to do it again. *Ignite Azusa* is one of these books. Jennifer A. Miskov has captured what the Spirit of God started at Azusa Street in the early 1900s, and has made it available for us to experience it today. The greatest awakening is knocking at our door. The day of Psalm 110:3 is upon us as a generation and God's people will volunteer freely on the day of His power. As you read *Ignite Azusa*, I pray that your heart is ignited with the fiery presence of God and that you press in for all that God has for you in our generation.

MARK BROOKES
Senior Overseer for 1st Year
Bethel School of Supernatural Ministry

In *Ignite Azusa*, the Holy Spirit is waiting to encounter your heart with a new wave of faith and expectancy for what God is doing in our generation. Jennifer A. Miskov has a way of partnering with the Holy Spirit to create an atmosphere where you will actually encounter the God of Revival. When I read *Ignite Azusa*, I found myself having to stop frequently to engage with God. The Holy Spirit was piercing my heart and marking me with a deeper hunger. *Ignite Azusa* deepened my burning passion to be consecrated to Jesus in a new way; it brought alignment in my life to be positioned for what He is preparing for us right now. Throughout the book, it's almost as if God is saying, "The time is now! Get ready!" When you read *Ignite Azusa*, you can expect to walk away powerfully touched and changed by the exact same God who shook up Azusa.

JESSIKA TATE
Bethel School of Supernatural Ministry student

DEDICATION

This book is dedicated to all of the spiritual mothers and fathers who have believed in me, discipled me, championed me, created space for me to shine, or sown into my life in one way or another over the years. I would not be where I am today without your friendship and investment in my life.

Jamie Gillentine, your life has always been such a great example of what the love of Jesus looks like here on earth. Thank you for teaching me that through the spiritual disciplines, I could have greater access into the heart of God. Greg Allen, thanks for seeing the gold in me and creating space for me to preach when I was just a teenager. Bob and Penny Fulton, I would not be where I am today without all of your prayers and support. Bob, thank you for loving for me, imparting your wisdom, teaching me how to disciple others, and demonstrating the importance of fighting for community. Van and Joyce Pewthers, your faithful prayers and love for me have always made coming to visit feel like home.

Mark Cartledge, I am so blessed by you and your incredible family. Thank you for the pastoral role you played in my life when I lived in England, as well as your mentorship in my studies. Your family's constant love and support in my life is such gold to me. The McNeils, the Inksters, and so many others have also been a great blessing to me while I lived in England.

Bernie Ooley, thank you for believing in me and creating space for me to impart the significance of revival history to so many. You are a door opener who champions and helps launch many into their destinies. Stephen DeSilva, God has used you to save my life by restoring hope to me during a very challenging season. For this, I will always be grateful. God has greatness in store for you that will astonish you. Mark Brookes, it has been a dream come true to teach revival history alongside of you at Bethel School of Supernatural Ministry. The way that you love, lead, and raise up revivalists in this generation through the joy of the Father impacts more than you know.

Bill Johnson, thank you for the way that you host God's presence and burn for revival. You have paved the way for many to follow. I am so grateful that you invited me to partner with you on *Defining Moments*. It has marked my life. Your generosity and love for the body of Christ is life-changing. Lou Engle, my heart is stirred by your passion and consecration for God. It is such an honor to meet a fellow well digger. I am inspired to burn for God more because of your life.

Heidi Baker, you have impacted me more than you realize. Your love for Jesus stirs a hunger deep inside of me for more of God. I was inspired by the love of Jesus in you the first day I met you over sixteen years ago. I am so grateful for the way you have championed and supported me in my destiny. Your friendship has given me courage to step out in faith like never before. The way that you have loved and believed in me has changed my life.

And even though I have never personally met Carrie Judd Montgomery, I also dedicate this book to her. She has taught me how to live above circumstances and how to dream for the impossible. She has shown me what it means to walk by faith and not by sight and to value living in God's all-consuming presence as a lifestyle.

For all of these and the many more who have impacted me over the years, I pray that the fruit from my life would be multiplied and added to your inheritance. May every single breakthrough, promise fulfilled, and life that is changed be added to your legacy and release overflowing blessings for the investment you have made in my life.

SPECIAL THANKS

I am so grateful to Heidi Baker, Lou Engle, and Bill Johnson for partnering with me to release this important story. David Stoddard's attention to detail, value for excellence, and partnership with the Holy Spirit has brought a wonderful book cover to life. Thanks to Daystar Frady, Uta Schmidt, Mark Cartledge, Vinson Synan, Dennis Flom, Glenn Gohr, Glory Eshareturi, Jonathan McGraw, Cathy Sanders, and others who have helped by transcribing interviews, editing, or giving me feedback on this project. Your help and insights were invaluable. Thanks to those at the Christian and Missionary Alliance Archive Center and the Flower Pentecostal Heritage Center for your help with the photographs used in this book. *Ignite Azusa* would not have been possible without the prayers and support of Kristy Tillman, Mark Brookes, Mike and Yvonne Thomas, Keong Leong, Saint Mark, the Destiny House family, and so many more of my family and friends. Thank you so much! And of course I am thankful for the Holy Spirit inspiring not only this story, but also the story that was initiated over a hundred years ago at a house on Bonnie Brae Street.

NOTE TO THE READER

This book is not intended to give an in-depth historical treatment of the Azusa Street Revival because there are already many out there who have done incredible work and research to bring these details to life.[1] Rather, this book is meant to provide a very brief overview and snapshot of the revival and a few of the events leading up to it. By exploring the Azusa Street Revival, we can then tap into the prophetic inheritance of what God did over one hundred years ago, and grow in expectation of what He wants to do in even greater measures in our day.

7

CONTENTS

THE CURRENT OF REVIVAL IS SWEEPING BY OUR DOOR

It is not an accident that you are holding *Ignite Azusa* in your hands right now. Divine destiny is awaiting you in these pages. The fire from the Azusa Street Revival is still burning and available today. The Azusa Street Revival was not just something that happened over a hundred years ago, it prophesies into our future about what God wants to pour out in even greater measures today. This book will reignite your passion for more of God and help position you to step into the fullness of your God-given destiny for such a time as this. It will equip you to steward the next outpouring of the Spirit with greater wisdom and insight.

We are on the brink of something beautiful that we have never seen before. We have been given the incredible opportunity to step into something truly special in our generation. There is momentum that has already been created for us to tap into by those at Azusa. Lessons and keys for our destiny are embedded in their story. We can access these to unlock even greater realms of God's glory in our day.

In the first part of *Ignite Azusa*, the Azusa story will be told along with some of the main themes that emerged. Part two is about positioning ourselves to build upon the momentum of what God did at Azusa. We will explore more of what it means to partner with God in helping this next generation break into their destiny. Following this are several keys for stewarding this next move of God well so that we can continue to burn for Jesus all our days and not burn out. Wisdom and impartation from three of my personal heroes, Heidi Baker, Lou Engle, and Bill Johnson, will also be included. As you go on this journey exploring more about the Azusa Street Revival, I pray that a fire will be ignited in your heart to burn for Jesus like never before.

ON THE HORIZON

Many have prophesied about a new move of God on the horizon that far surpasses any we have ever seen. In his book *Ever Increasing Faith* (1924), the famous British evangelist Smith Wigglesworth (1859-1947) prophesied of a greater revival to come when he said, "I believe that this Pentecostal revival that we are now in is the best thing that the Lord has on the earth today, and yet I believe that God has something out of this that is going to be still better."[2]

Later, Wigglesworth gave South African born David du Plessis (1905-1987) a personal prophecy about the coming of a great move of God that would overshadow all others. David du Plessis said that one morning in December of 1936, Wigglesworth burst into his office to share about "a revival that will eclipse anything we have known throughout history." Wigglesworth said, "No such things have happened in times past as will happen when this begins…It will eclipse the present-day, twentieth-century Pentecostal revival that already is a marvel to the world." He continued by revealing how the Pentecostal movement would be "a light thing in comparison with what God will do through the old churches. There will be tremendous gatherings of people, unlike anything we've seen."[3]

On August 8, 1975, prophet Bob Jones had an encounter with the Lord in a death experience where he was taken into heaven. God asked him and the others near him one question: "Did you learn to love?" When Bob was about to respond that he had, he heard the Lord say to him, "Go back because I'm going to bring a billion souls unto Myself in one great wave and I want you to touch a few of the leaders that I am going to use in that time."[4]

Both Smith Wigglesworth and Bob Jones have since gone to be with the Lord, but their prophecies live on. Countless other similar prophecies have also been released, all pointing toward the same message: a greater awakening than any we have ever seen is on the horizon.

So what if these and the many other prophecies are true and we really are on the tipping point of a billion-soul harvest? What if our generation is pregnant with birthing the next Great Awakening? What if a new Jesus Revolution is just around the corner? Wouldn't you like to be a part of God crashing into this generation and partnering to bring in the greatest harvest in history? *Ignite Azusa* is written to help position you to step into the greatest move of God yet to come, and to ignite a fire of love and passion for Jesus that can't be quenched.

The Azusa Street Revival (1906-1909) was a significant spiritual awakening that played a crucial role in the emergence of Pentecostalism and the rapid growth of Christianity around the globe. This move of God has brought more people to Jesus than in centuries past. On November 16, 1905, just months before the revival was sparked in California, an intercessor in Los Angeles named Frank Bartleman felt a stirring similar to what many of us might be feeling today. He said,

> The current of revival is sweeping by our door. Will we cast ourselves on its mighty bosom and ride to glorious victory? A year of life at this time, with its wonderful possibilities for God, is worth a hundred years of ordinary life. "Pentecost" is knocking at our doors. The revival for our country is no longer a question. Slowly but surely the tide has been rising until in the very near future we believe for a deluge of salvation that will sweep all before it. Wales will not long stand alone in this glorious triumph for our Christ. The spirit of reviving is coming upon us, driven by the breath of God, the Holy Ghost. The clouds are gathering rapidly, big with a mighty rain, whose precipitation lingers but a little.

Heroes will arise from the dust of obscure and despised circumstances, whose names will be emblazoned on Heaven's eternal page of fame. The Spirit is brooding over our land again as at creation's dawn, and the fiat of God goes forth. "Let there be light." Brother, sister, if we all believed God can you realize what would happen? Many of us here are living for nothing else. A volume of believing prayer is ascending to the throne night and day. Los Angeles, Southern California, and the whole continent shall surely find itself ere long in the throes of a mighty revival, by the Spirit and power of God.[5]

Can you feel the stirring deep within your spirit? If we really believed God, can you realize what might happen? Many of us today are sensing the intensity and weight of what God is about to pour out in all the earth. We are indeed on the verge of the greatest revival we have ever seen. The momentum of those who have gone before us is great.

As you dive into the Azusa story, I declare that the weak be made strong, the hidden unveiled, the broken-hearted restored and made whole, and the wounded healed. I call forth the heroes to arise from the dust of obscure and despised circumstances. As you read *Ignite Azusa*, I pray that the Holy Spirit will ignite you with the fire of God like never before.

God, do it again in our day and even more. Whatever it looks like, we don't care, just as long as we have more of You. Release the keys of intimacy and destiny that You want to deposit into our generation. Overshadow us and cause us to burn for You with a flame that will never go out. We are Yours forever, Lord. Mark us for your glory. We say yes to You, no matter what the cost.

PART ONE

1

CATCHING THE WAVE
OF THE SPIRIT

TAPPING INTO THE CURRENTS OF REVIVAL

This is what the Lord says: "Stand at the crossroads and look; ask
for the ancient paths, ask where the good way is, and walk in it,
and you will find rest for your souls."

Jeremiah 6:16

Tapping into the power of the testimony is a critical part of
partnering with God to fulfill all that He has called us to do
and to become; it is essential for stepping into our fullest destiny in Him. Releasing a testimony is recounting or retelling
a story of how God moved in one's life. In remembering the
history of God, faith is released in the atmosphere. In the Hebrew language, the word *testimony* is derived from a root word,
which means, "to do again."[6] Sharing a testimony creates an
atmosphere for the sign, wonder, or miracle to be duplicated.
In essence, sharing a testimony is about wanting God to do it
again. If prophecy causes change in present events, releasing a
testimony is pulling from the past to prophesy a greater future.

One of the weightiest mistakes one generation of the Israelites
made was when they forgot the testimonies of what God had
done on their behalf (Numbers 13). Disregarding God's faith-
fulness caused one whole generation to miss out on their des-

tiny. They forgot how God had parted the Red Sea and done the impossible for them. This slight amnesia caused them to lose sight of God's goodness when the time came for them to possess the Promised Land. Instead of finding the courage to move forward by recounting what God had done in the past, they allowed fear of the giants to sabotage their chance to take possession of the Promised Land. God wanted them to remember what He had done on their behalf because He knew that it would strengthen and help propel them into a new and greater season.

Learning to tap into the currents of revival and the power of the testimony is like surfing. I grew up bodyboarding and surfing in Newport Beach, California. This beach has jetties—or rock piles—spaced along the coast every four blocks to prevent the shoreline from erosion and to channel the currents. If surfers do not know this surf spot, they might paddle out in the middle of the two jetties. Because they are unaware of the landscape and the currents, it will take that person much longer to paddle out to get to the big waves. They will hopefully still make it out, but they will be more exhausted and it will take them twice as long to get there. They will also receive a greater pounding on their paddle out and have to overcome more resistance. However, the locals know that the best place to paddle out is right next to the jetty, because it has an unseen current there. They know that this current will take them out to the big waves with minimal paddling and duck diving (going under oncoming waves). This choice may look dangerous to the onlooker because it is so near the rocks. However, because the locals know the currents, they will make it out to the big waves using half the energy and in half the time. They have learned the art of tapping into the specific currents that will get them to the big waves.

This is the beauty of the power of the testimony. It is simply tapping into the faith currents of those who have gone before to launch us out even further into the big waves of what God is doing in our generation. We can pull not only from Scripture and prophetic words, but also from testimonies of those who have gone before us—including those at the Azusa Street Revival. We can build on their momentum and ride in their faith stream to deeper breakthrough and greater destiny. When we discover the currents of those who have come before us, we won't have to paddle so hard. Tapping into these faith streams can take us farther than we could go on our own. They can take us deeper in God than we've ever known. They can make us brave.

A RADICAL WAVE APPROACHING CALIFORNIA
by Heidi Baker

I believe God has His eye on California. The Golden State is full of pioneers. So many great things that are happening around the world started there. It is interesting that the Azusa Street Revival, which was a major center for the Pentecostal movement, Calvary Chapel, The Vineyard, and other radical missions movements, all started in California.

I was born in Newport Beach, California and grew up on a private beach in Laguna Beach. It was a beautiful place to be.

I would go bodyboarding and surfing all the time. I felt so at home in the water and I learned so much about the Holy Spirit through surfing. Before I would catch a wave, I first had to paddle hard to position myself correctly. Then once I caught the wave, I had to yield myself completely to the flow of the ocean. I then entered into a moment of total surrender and delight as the wave carried me.

Surfing is a lot like life in the Holy Spirit. Sometimes we have to work and paddle hard to get in the right position. Then when God shows up, everything changes. We catch the wave of His Spirit and He takes us wherever He wills. We simply need to let go of all control, cling tight to Him, and enjoy the ride. God is the one who is in control of the wave.

I believe there is going to be another wave of the Spirit in California. That's why the enemy wants to get the church to leave. I have heard of warnings telling people to leave California because of coming disasters. That's the worst thing to do in my opinion because if we die, we're in the glory and with Jesus. What's the problem with that? If we want to catch the wave of the Spirit, even if there's a disaster in California, where would we rather be? Wouldn't we want to carry the glory of God when things get rough?

California is getting ready for another radical wave of revival. I want to call the church to come to California and to catch that wave. When disasters strike or things shake or earthquakes hit, that's a perfect time to be the answer the world needs and to demonstrate God's love. Jesus spoke to me and said, "I died so there would always be enough." That's also true for California no matter what happens. I want to encourage people to come to California, to get ready for the next wave, and to ride it for His glory.

DIGGING THE WELLS
OF REVIVAL IN CALIFORNIA
by Lou Engle

A few years back, I visited Carrie Judd Montgomery's healing home in Oakland, California, called the Home of Peace. When I was at this historic revival well, the host showed me the guest book from 1908 with an entry by Azusa Street Revival participant Frank Bartleman. Although I have never met Bartleman, he has always been like a spiritual father for me because of his deep passion for intercession to see revival. I feel he is up there in the great cloud of witnesses encouraging me on in these days. I discovered that he wrote out his own modified version of Isaiah 59:16 in the guest book: "And He saw that there was no man, and wondered that there was no intercession."[7] I felt the Lord say to me, "Let San Francisco and California have an intercessor right now." Not long after, my team and I decided to spend our forty-day fast for TheCall Berkeley at the Home of Peace in 2014.

Just as Bartleman interceded before the birth of the Azusa Street Revival because he could sense a historic shift, so I believe that we are also at a tipping point in our generation. It will be important to draw from the well at Azusa Street to gain insights on how we can better partner with what God wants to do in our day and go even further. When California seeks God like they sought for gold in the early days, God's glory will return.

I pray for each one reading *Ignite Azusa* that you would have encounters and open heaven visitations. I pray for revival days to explode and that God would restore the breech, and repair the fallen down walls and city streets' dwellings. I pray that God would pour out His Spirit like He did during Lonnie Frisbee's time and that there would be another wave of revival in California, a new Jesus Movement. I pray that each one reading this book would have an encounter with God that will set the next stage of history in California, in America, and beyond.

PRAYER TO BE IGNITED

by Bill Johnson

California has a wonderful history with God, and one of its finest moments was the Azusa Street Revival. The people at Azusa Street burned for more of Jesus, and a global revival came forth. Personal and corporate revival doesn't come without that inner burning. This fire can't be ignited by visions or ambitions alone. It's got to be because the Spirit of God comes on you. You just have to burn.

So I ask, Father, that You would release a grace over all who read *Ignite Azusa*. Let there be an igniting encounter like on the road to Emmaus when the men were walking along with Jesus talking to Him and they said, "Did not our hearts burn?" I pray for burning hearts, ablaze with love for the Son. Set people up for divine encounters. Let there not be a person who is without the fire of God.

God, we invite You to come display yourself powerfully. Do what only You can do. God, we give You that place. We honor and celebrate You. Our love is for You. Lord, I pray that You would raise up a generation that knows what purity is and knows what power is and walks in both well. I ask that for the honor of the name Jesus.

2

PIONEERS WHO
PAVED THE WAY

California has deep wells of revival to draw from. There is a great inheritance to be found by accessing the wells in this land. It is in digging these wells that we can intersect a stream of living water that is freely accessible for us today. Waters of the Holy Spirit attract heaven. Wells of revival draw us closer to the Source of living water and inspire us to dig even deeper.[8]

The deep well of the Azusa Street Revival that sprung forth at the turn of the twentieth century has impacted Christianity in a major way. Most, though not all, Pentecostal and charismatic churches (or those influenced by these) can eventually trace their roots back to Azusa Street in one way or another. By accessing the riches of what God has done in the past, we can position ourselves to step into even more of His glory in our day. Before we look deeper into the well at Los Angeles, let's first look at a few of the forerunners and see what God was doing around the world at the turn of the twentieth century leading up to the revival. This way we can better understand where we are in history right now and what God has in store for us in the coming awakening.

CHARLES F. PARHAM:
DISCOVERING NEW CURRENTS

Charles F. Parham

Charles Fox Parham (1873-1929) is known for being a forerunner and a key influencer of the theology of the Pentecostal movement. He started a ministry school in Topeka, Kansas, with the intention to teach students how to seek the presence of the Holy Spirit in a greater way so they could prepare to evangelize the world with greater power from on high. The school was founded in an old mansion that looked like a castle called Stone's Folly. One of the two towers was converted into a prayer tower where students prayed on rotation for twenty-four hours a day.

When Parham went on a trip toward the end of 1900, he left the students with the assignment of searching the Scriptures to find the proof and evidence of being baptized in the Holy Spirit. When he returned, they had decided that the answer was speaking in tongues. Then on New Year's Eve of 1900, a student named Agnes Ozman asked Parham to lay hands on her and pray for her to receive the Spirit baptism with the evidence of speaking in tongues.[9] In the early hours of the first day of the new century on January 1, 1901, Ozman spoke in tongues for the first time. That same week Parham and many of the students also began to speak in tongues.[10] Giving a pre-history to the workings at Azusa Street, this unknown author (possibly William J. Seymour himself) wrote about Parham's work, saying that it began

[W]hen a company of people under the leadership of Chas. Parham, who were studying God's word tarried for Pentecost, in Topeka, Kansas. After searching through the country everywhere, they had been unable to find any Christians that had the true Pentecostal power. So they laid aside all commentaries and notes and waited on the Lord, studying His word, and what they did not understand they got down before the bench and asked God to have wrought out in their hearts by the Holy Ghost. They had a prayer tower in which prayers were ascending night and day to God. After three months, a sister who had been teaching sanctification for the baptism with the Holy Ghost, one who had a sweet, loving experience and all the carnality taken out of her heart, felt the Lord lead her to have hands laid on her to receive the Pentecost. So when they prayed, the Holy Ghost came in great power and she commenced speaking in an unknown tongue. [11]

This was at a time when speaking in tongues was unheard of. This was a major breakthrough for that generation. Parham taught a new understanding of Spirit baptism that was a separate experience from sanctification. His theology will be important and come into play as the Azusa story develops.

PANDITA RAMABAI: FIRE FALLS IN INDIA (1905)

In the early part of the twentieth century, revival fires began to break out around the globe, sometimes connected to each

other and sometimes not. It was as if the early twentieth century was sacred time for God to do a new thing in the whole earth.[12] A few years after the breakthrough at Parham's school, Wales experienced a mighty revival. Not long after God began pouring out His Spirit in Wales, Pandita Ramabai also experienced revival at her orphanage in Mukti, India in 1905.

Pandita Ramabai

Pandita Ramabai (1858-1922) started a home in 1895 to rescue young women who were left destitute as a result of child marriages or widowhood. By 1900, she had taken in up to 2,000 people because of a famine that hit the land. She especially helped Hindu women realize that they could have new life in Christ. In early 1905, Ramabai felt a stirring to begin praying for revival. She shared her hunger for revival with others and enlisted seventy people to join her in her efforts. Shortly after this, 550 people met two times a day to pray.[13]

Then on June 29, 1905 at 3:00 a.m., the Holy Spirit fell on one of Ramabai's volunteers. American missionary Minnie Abrams recorded the story saying that

> The young woman sleeping next to her awoke when this occurred, and seeing the fire enveloping her, ran across the dormitory, brought a pail of water and was about to dash it upon her, when she discovered that she was not on fire. In less than an hour nearly all of the young women in the compound gathered around, weeping, praying, and confessing their sins to God. The newly Spirit baptized girl sat in the midst of them, telling what God had done for her and exhorting them to repentance.[14]

The very next day, Ramabai was teaching from John 8 in her "usual quiet way" when the Holy Spirit stirred up intense intercession amongst the girls so much that Ramabai had to stop talking. The room was filled with the "presence of God" and many were weeping and praying, hungering after God. Immediately following this, prayer meetings took over the center so much that even school classes were suspended. Many experienced a deep burning of the fire of the Holy Spirit, causing them to realize at a deep level the price Jesus paid for them. This was followed by a great joy of their salvation.[15] Ramabai eventually urged the students in her Bible school to give up their "secular" studies so that they could preach the gospel in the neighboring villages. Thirty women responded to this call and began to pray daily with each other for "more of Jesus."[16]

EVAN ROBERTS AND
THE WELSH REVIVAL (1904-1905)

Evan Roberts

Hunger for God was increasing around the world at the start of the twentieth century. Wales experienced a mighty outpouring of the Holy Spirit from 1904 -1905 when God raised up a coal miner in his twenties named Evan Roberts (1878-1951). In less than four months, over 100,000 people got saved. Shops closed down, people reconciled, crime decreased, debts were paid off, and the nation was brought to a spiritual awakening which continues to have ripple effects around the world to this day.

When this revival burst upon the scene, people from around the world were drawn to Wales to partake in what God was doing. They did not come to see an anointed speaker or a talented worship band on a stage; they came to meet with God. One eyewitness recounts:

> I saw a large, deep gallery surrounding the chapel literally packed with men. They were manly, intensely earnest faces, not looking around or talking one to the other, but with one consent utterly taken up with God. The body of the chapel was also crowded with men and women of all classes, with but one purpose–TO MEET GOD. There was no opening to the meeting; the hearts were full, and burst with prayer and praise to a God felt to be in our midst.[17]

The meetings were marked by prayer, testimony, and worship. The spontaneous leading of the Holy Spirit took precedent over any set plans or agendas. People were drawn to this revival to encounter God in a greater measure than ever before. While there were many factors that contributed to the Azusa Street

Revival, one to highlight is the unique connection it had with the Welsh Revival.

JOSEPH SMALE: A BAPTIST MINISTER
GETS MARKED BY GOD IN WALES

In 1905, a Baptist pastor in Los Angeles who was originally from England, went on a sabbatical to visit the revival in Wales. Joseph Smale (1867-1926) was impacted by the fullness of God's presence in that place. He returned home and was on fire to see the same outpouring released in his home city.[18] He immediately changed his style of preaching and did revival meetings every night, patterned after the meetings he experienced in Wales.[19] The board of The First Baptist Church he pastored didn't like his new direction and eventually confronted him. He resigned and went on to found The First New Testament Church in Los Angeles.

Joseph Smale

Intercessor Frank Bartleman crossed paths with Smale and saw that God had begun to move in a special way at his church after his return from Wales. In June 1905, Bartleman noticed that "the Spirit has broken out" in Los Angeles as people were "rallying from all over the city to the meetings at Pastor Smale's church." As the Spirit was leading the meetings, people were getting saved and stirred up for revival. Bartleman said "the fear of God is coming upon the people, a very spirit of burning."[20] Many of the night meetings went on until the early morning hours of the next day.

Bartleman wrote about one meeting he attended at Smale's church where God crashed in on them in a powerful way.

> One night at the New Testament Church, during a deep spirit of prayer on the congregation, the Lord came suddenly so near that we could feel His presence as though he were closing in on us around the edges of the meeting. Two-thirds of the people sprang to their feet in alarm, and some ran hurriedly out of the house, even leaving their hats behind them, almost scared out of their senses. There was no demonstration in the natural out of the ordinary to cause this fright. It was a supernatural manifestation of His nearness. What would such do if they saw the Lord.[21]

The impartation from the Welsh Revival began to spread in Los Angeles, in part because of this Baptist minister who had a burning passion to see revival in his city. An *impartation* is like a spiritual deposit or a transfer of blessing from one person or community to another to release a similar effect or impact.[22]

FRANK BARTLEMAN:
PREGNANT WITH INTERCESSION

Intercessor Frank Bartleman (1871-1936) burned to see revival break out in Los Angeles in the early 1900s. He also recognized that God was doing something special in Wales so he spread testimonies of the Welsh Revival to create hunger for more of God in his city.[23] In May 1905, he wrote in an article, "My soul is on fire as I read of the glorious work of grace in Wales…But where are the men who will 'stir themselves up to take hold on God?' Let our watchword at this time be 'California for Christ.'"[24] He believed that God was doing something special in California at that time and wanted to both invite it and position himself to catch the wave.

> Slowly but surely the conviction is coming upon the saints of Southern California that God is going to pour out His Spirit here as in Wales.

We are having faith for things such as we have never dreamed of, for the near future. We are assured of no less than a "Pentecost" for this whole country. But we can never have pentecostal results without pentecostal power. And this will mean pentecostal demonstration. Few care to meet God face to face.[25]

Bartleman carried a burden of intercession for his city that was so strong that he "cried out like a woman in birth-pangs."[26] God would encounter him mightily during these times of intercession. One time in deep prayer he said that

A heaven of divine love filled and thrilled my soul. Burning fire went through me. In fact my whole being seemed to flow down before Him, like wax before the fire. I lost all consciousness of time or space, being conscious only of His wonderful presence. I worshipped at His feet.[27]

Another time when he was praying at a house meeting, he said that God "came and filled our little cottage with a cloud of glory until I could scarcely bear His presence."[28]

Bartleman was an intercessor at his core. He felt things in the Spirit even when he didn't see them in the natural and then he took them to the Lord in prayer. When praying, there were times when he felt as if he was experiencing birth pangs as a woman would feel in labor. Bartleman partnered in intercession to invite one of the greatest moves of God in history. He also later stewarded

Frank Bartleman

testimonies by writing them down and spreading them. His prayers helped to build momentum, expectation, and hunger for what God wanted to do in Los Angeles.

When a pregnant woman feels birth pangs, it is a sign that there is a baby inside that is about to come out soon. The most important thing for her to do in this season is to steward her body well, prepare and position herself, and wait for the right timing to push. Bartleman recognized that his generation was pregnant with birthing one of the greatest revivals anyone had seen up until that point. He partnered in prayer to help bring its release. Another way he partnered with God to love Los Angeles was by inviting impartation from another nation that had just given birth to a beautiful revival.

EVAN ROBERTS PRAYS FOR CALIFORNIA

Frank Bartleman was so captivated by what God was doing in Wales that he wrote to its primary leader, Evan Roberts, to ask for prayer for impartation for the same to happen in California. Roberts responded by committing to pray for a similar outpouring to be released in California and included directions of what to do next. Roberts commissioned Bartleman to

> Congregate the people together who are willing to make a total surrender. Pray and wait. Believe God's promises. Hold daily meetings. May God bless you, is my earnest prayer. Yours in Christ, Evan Roberts.[29]

In another letter to Bartleman, Roberts prophesied of a coming wave of revival that would surpass what God was doing in Wales.

> I believe that the world is upon the threshold of a great religious revival, and pray daily that I may be allowed to help bring this about. Wonderful things have happened in Wales in a few weeks, but these are only a beginning. The world will be swept by His Spirit as by a rushing, mighty wind. Many who are now silent Christians will lead the movement. They will see a great light, and will reflect this light to thousands now in darkness. Thousands will do more than we have accomplished, as God gives them power.[30]

Bartleman partnered together with Roberts in prayer for God to move in California. When two or more agree in prayer, God loves to act on their behalf (Matthew 18:18-20). It didn't matter that they were oceans apart; they were unified in spirit and both going after revival. Bartleman was wise in asking Roberts to pray for the same outpouring in Wales to overflow to Los Angeles. He believed in the prayer of impartation and that what God was doing in Wales could also break out in California.

Bartleman and Smale contributed to welcoming impartation of the Welsh Revival to the very doorstep of Los Angeles. While Smale went to Wales and brought back impartation to his whole community and city, Bartleman entreated its leader to pray for California. Both Smale and Bartleman held meetings and distributed literature about the Welsh Revival to churches throughout the Los Angeles area.[31] They believed that the momentum created in Wales would soon hit the shores of California.[32]

Just as Charles Finney sent his intercessor Daniel Nash ahead of him to pray and break up the fallow ground in cities before he came to preach, so Bartleman, Smale, and others were sent ahead to Los Angeles to pray before the incoming revival. God used these intercessors and others to prepare for a great outpouring of the Spirit before William J. Seymour came onto the scene.[33]

We have a lot we can learn from these pioneers in preparing for the next great awakening. They did more than just sit around and wait for the wave of revival to come. They partnered with God in prayer and intercession, and sought for impartation from those who were already experiencing more of what they were longing for.

Do you know of a particular move of God that is happening elsewhere that is similar to what you want to happen in your own life, family, church, or city? Consider visiting that place. If that is not possible, ask for someone from there to pray for you. Or invite someone from there to share with your community and release impartation. Ask God for ways you can partner with Him in your own life, family, and city through impartation and then act on what He shows you.

3

THE AZUSA
STREET STORY

WILLIAM J. SEYMOUR:
CATALYST FOR A GENERATION

William J. Seymour

African-American William Joseph Seymour (1870-1922) would eventually build upon the momentum in Los Angeles to become the catalyst and leader for the Azusa Street Revival. Born in Louisiana to parents who were at one time slaves, he taught himself how to read by studying the Bible. When he was in his twenties, he moved to Indianapolis where he made a commitment to Christ at a Methodist Episcopal Church.[34] Eventually Seymour moved to Chicago, Illinois, in 1900 and shortly after to Cincinnati, Ohio. There he was influenced by preacher Martin Wells Knapp, whose focus was on holiness and living a sanctified life, and who also embraced racial integration.[35] Because the Methodist churches he attended started to allow racial divides to enter in, he later joined a holiness group where he was "sanctified" and received his call to ministry. At this point in time, many holiness groups believed in a second work of grace that followed conversion called a sanctification experience, meaning that they were set apart for God in a new way.[36] At that time, many called this second blessing experience their baptism of the Holy Spirit.

Seymour came down with smallpox, which blinded him in one eye. He later believed God used his illness to cause him to step into the fullness of his calling.[37] After going to Houston, Texas, in 1902-1903 to connect with family, he felt led to go to Jackson, Mississippi, in the winter of 1904-1905 to seek counsel from a leader there about the direction of his call.[38] During this time and even before, Seymour was a deeply devout man. John G. Lake remembered Seymour to have said,

> Prior to my meeting with Parham, the Lord had sanctified me from sin, and had led me into a deep life of prayer, assigning five hours out of the twenty-four every day for prayer. This prayer life I continued for three and a half years, when one day as I prayed the Holy Ghost said to me, "There are better things to be had in the spiritual life, but they must be sought out with faith and prayer." This so quickened my soul that I increased my hours of prayer to seven out of twenty-four and continued to pray on for two years longer, until the baptism fell on us.[39]

INTERSECTING CHARLES PARHAM

In 1905, Seymour returned to Houston. In August of that year, he took over a Holiness congregation that his friend Lucy Farrow turned over to him so that she could serve as a governess for Charles Parham. In late 1905, Parham came to Houston and opened a Bible school to teach people about the newer theology of baptism of the Holy Spirit that included speaking in tongues. Farrow accompanied Parham and encouraged Seymour to attend his Bible school.

Parham's Bible School in Houston, Texas where Seymour attended classes in early 1906 and learned about the Pentecostal Spirit baptism experience. This was located at 503 Rusk Avenue on the corner of Rusk Avenue and Brazos Street.

In January 1906, even though segregation was prominent, Parham allowed Seymour, a black Holiness preacher, to attend his school. Because of the "Jim Crow" laws prevalent during that time, Seymour had to sit outside of Parham's classroom while the white students sat inside. Parham's decision to allow Seymour to attend his school was still radical at that time. Parham refused to turn away anyone who was hungry to learn—no matter the color of his or her skin. Parham would also minister together regularly with Seymour in the African-American communities nearby. Seymour looked up to Parham as a spiritual father at this time. It was also under Parham's teaching that Seymour learned about speaking in tongues as initial evidence—or proof—of the baptism of the Holy Spirit.

INVITATION TO THE CITY OF ANGELS

A woman named Neely Terry from Julia W. Hutchins' small Holiness mission in Los Angeles visited Seymour while he was pastoring a church in Houston. It was through this connection that in February 1906, Hutchins invited Seymour to come to preach, and hopefully to pastor, so she could go to the mission field in Africa.

Prior to this, Hutchins, along with about eight other families, were kicked out of the Second Baptist Church in Los Angeles because they embraced the new Holiness theology of a second work of grace. As a result, they decided to hold prayer and Bible study meetings at Richard and Ruth Asberry's home at 214 Bonnie Brae Street to continue in their pursuit for more of God. When meetings got too big at the home, Hutchins opened up a mission at Ninth and Santa Fe Street. This was the same church she invited Seymour to pastor.[40]

Los Angeles was a melting pot for different cultures and nationalities at that time. The population of around 230,000 people was growing at a rate of 15 percent per year. At first, Parham did not want Seymour to go to Los Angeles. However, because Seymour's conviction to go was so strong, he later supported him on his journey. Seymour left Houston around February 18 and arrived in the City of Angels on February 22, 1906. Two days later, he preached to Hutchins' congregation about Spirit baptism as a third work of grace, freely available to anyone who hungered for it. This newer theology that Seymour had learned from Parham was offensive to many Christians because they believed they had already been baptized in the Holy Spirit when they had a second blessing or sanctification experience. Many of them associated the term *Spirit baptism* with their sanctification experience. When this new teaching was released, they felt it discounted their previous understanding of already having had a Spirit baptism encounter. Seymour taught about this fresh encounter being added to and building upon previous experiences, not negating them. He preached about and encouraged others to have this new Spirit baptism experience with the sign of speaking in tongues before he ever spoke in tongues himself.

Because of Seymour's teaching, Hutchins locked him out of her mission on Sunday March 4. He did not have enough money to go back to Houston and didn't know what to do next. Luckily, Edward S. Lee, a member of Hutchins' church, invited Seymour over for lunch and opened his home for him to stay so he wouldn't be left stranded in the streets. In this time of desperation for a greater outpouring of the Holy Spirit, Seymour, Lee, and others planned a ten day fast where they would read Acts 2:1-4 and pray every evening until they had the same experience the disciples had at Pentecost.[42]

Lee and Seymour grew hungry to see God move. When Lee returned from work, they would pray together.[43] People began to seek Seymour out in the Lee home. Despite the resistance he encountered by the leadership who invited him there, Seymour was relentless in seeking the outpouring of the Holy Spirit as promised in the book of Acts. This little group who were hungry for more of God "became determined to receive their Pentecost 'at all costs', sometimes praying all night long."[44] The prayer meetings grew in size so they had to move them two blocks away to Richard and Ruth Asberry's house at 214 North Bonnie Brae Street.[45]

BONNIE BRAE HOUSE

In those early meetings at the Asberry house on Bonnie Brae Street, there were only about fifteen people including children, many of them coming from Hutchins' mission.[46] Even though Seymour had yet to receive the "evidence" of speaking in tongues, he continued to teach about it. On April 9, 1906, just before leaving for the prayer meeting, Edward Lee began to speak in tongues after Seymour laid hands on and prayed for him. After this, Lee, Seymour, and the others walked the couple blocks up the street to the Asberry home on Bonnie Brae Street for the 7:30 p.m. prayer meeting.[47]

The Asberry's house at 214 North Bonnie Brae Street around the time the revival was ignited. A few years later, the city changed the street number to 216 North Bonnie Brae Street. The home is open today for visitors and others who want to tap into the well of revival there.

There, a handful of African-American saints gathered together because they wanted to encounter God in a greater measure. They had a song, a few prayers, and several testimonies released. Seymour shared the testimony of how Lee spoke in tongues less than two hours before.[48] He then began to preach from Acts 2:4, how when the day of Pentecost had come, tongues of fire appeared upon the people and they were filled with the Holy Spirit, speaking in other tongues.[49]

Then something happened that they had all been waiting and longing for. God crashed into that meeting like never before and someone started to speak in tongues. Several others got baptized in the Holy Spirit and spoke in tongues as well. Ruth Asberry's cousin Jennie Evans Moore, who lived across the street, was resting on a stool, when she suddenly fell to the ground and began to speak in tongues. She is known as one of the first women in Los Angeles to speak in tongues during this time. She recalled that it felt like a vessel broke inside of her and water "surged" through her entire being. When this rush came to her

lips, she spoke in six different languages that she had seen earlier in a vision. These tongues were each interpreted in English.
Following this release, Jennie, who had never played the piano
before, walked over to the piano and played it under the anointing while singing in tongues.[50] She recounted the story in the
Azusa Mission's newspaper called *The Apostolic Faith.*

> For years before this wonderful experience came to us, we as a family,
> were seeking to know the fulnes of God, and He was filling us with
> His presence until we could hardly contain the power... On April 9,
> 1906, I was praising the Lord from the depths of my heart at home,
> and when the evening came and we attended the meeting the power
> of God fell and I was baptized in the Holy Ghost and fire, with the
> evidence of speaking in tongues...As I thought thereon and looked
> to God, it seemed as if a vessel broke within me and water surged
> up through my being, which when it reached my mouth came out
> in a torrent of speech in the languages which God had given me...I
> sang under the power of the Spirit in many languages, the interpreta-
> tion both words and music which I had never before heard, and in
> the home where the meeting was being held, the Spirit led me to the
> piano, where I played and sang under inspiration, although I had not
> learned to play.[51]

A few days later on April 12, 1906, Seymour spoke in tongues
for the first time after tarrying with a white brother and not
giving up until he "came through" at nearly four o'clock in
the morning.[52]

Frank Bartleman first learned about this new move of God
while at Smale's First New Testament Church on Easter Sunday morning April 15, when member Jennie Evans Moore came
to the service and spoke in tongues.[53] This created "a great stir"
with people there, who gathered in little groups after the service
on the sidewalk to try and figure out what this new "sign" might
mean. It was then that Bartleman discovered that "the Spirit
had fallen a few nights before, April 9, at the little cottage on
Bonnie Brae street."[54]

Crowds of both black and white people from Smale's First New Testament Church, Hutchins' mission, and other Holiness groups in the area came to the house on Bonnie Brae Street to see and partake in what God was doing. At one point, the house swelled with people so much that the front porch caved in. No one was injured, but they realized that they had outgrown the house and it was time to get a larger place. Within a week, they moved to a vacant building at 312 Azusa Street, which used to be a Methodist Episcopal church before it had been damaged by a fire.

AZUSA STREET MISSION

The day after the great San Francisco earthquake on April 18, 1906, Bartleman made his first visit to the Azusa Street Mission where he remembered there were about a "dozen saints there," with Seymour in charge.[55] Bartleman noticed that in that old dusty building, they had made seats out of planks for about thirty people, all arranged in a square so the people could face each other.[56] The way the seating was arranged in the early days facilitated an environment for the Holy Spirit to freely move without restrictions.

As word spread about how God was pouring out His Spirit in a powerful way, hundreds began to visit the Azusa Mission. They opened their doors to have continuous services every day to accommodate those who were hungry to meet with God.[57] This new all-encompassing encounter with God, which they called the baptism of the Spirit with speaking in tongues, drew people from around the world. Once participants had their Pentecostal Spirit baptism experience and spoke in tongues, they would readily testify and then return to their homes, releasing impartation to many.[58]

The building that became the Azusa Street Mission.

It is important to note that speaking in tongues was a new manifestation during their day. While it is more common today, it was a breakthrough sign and wonder in the early 1900s, recovering the gift that was manifest in the early church at Pentecost in the book of Acts. People who wanted a deeper encounter with God hungered for this new experience. Still others were drawn to the Mission at Azusa Street to criticize the movement, but were apprehended by God. Many times those who came to oppose the work of God at Azusa left having encountered God's love and speaking in tongues.

God encountered people powerfully in the Mission. Bartleman observed "in that old building, with its low rafters and bare floors, God took strong men and women to pieces, and put them together again, for His glory. It was a tremendous overhauling process."[59] It was normal to hear people shouting, crying, testifying, speaking in tongues, or interpreting tongues at the Azusa Mission. Because the building was only forty feet by sixty feet and was surrounded by stables, lumberyards, and tombstone businesses, they could get away with being as loud as they wanted, even into the late hours.[60]

No collections were taken at the Mission; there was just a box in the back that said, "Settle with the Lord."[61] While funds were not solicited, money came into the Mission and people were very generous. God provided time and time again for the early volunteers as they worked full time in leading people into the Pentecostal fullness, saving souls, praying for the sick, and ministering to those who came to the Mission.[62]

The flame of the Azusa Street Revival was first ignited when a small group of family and friends gathered together in a home and committed to seeking God until He met them in a powerful way. They knew there was more available to them and that speaking in tongues was possible because of those who had come before. When a handful of people unified together to encounter God in a more significant way than ever before, something was sparked that would later mark history. It doesn't take many people to start a fire. All that is needed is hunger and a burning relentlessness that will stop at nothing until God invades. What will you do with the hunger inside you? How will you cultivate it? Who else do you know who might also want to pursue greater depths of God's heart together?

4

ENCOUNTER

Encounter was at the heart of the Azusa Street Revival. People from around the world traveled thousands of miles to wait on the Lord to be endued with power from on high. They wanted to have an all-consuming encounter with God that would mark them for life.[64] The baptism of the Holy Spirit with the sign of speaking in tongues became the pearl of great price for those at Azusa.[65] People simply wanted to meet with God in those days. Frank Bartleman reported about the early meetings at Azusa,

> We were delivered right there from ecclesiastical hierarchism and abuse. We wanted God. When we first reached the meeting we avoided as much as possible human contact and greeting. We wanted to meet God first. We got our head under some bench in the corner in prayer, and met men only in the Spirit, knowing them "after the flesh" no more.[66]

Azusa was a revival of the Holy Spirit, inspired and informed by the disciples' experience at Pentecost in the book of Acts. After having a personal Pentecost experience, those at Azusa understood that speaking in tongues would follow. Speaking in tongues was different and weird; some even said it was from Satan. It didn't matter what it looked like though, the early saints at Azusa stopped at nothing to partake in all that God wanted to pour out in their generation, even if others criticized them.

CARRIE JUDD MONTGOMERY'S STORY

Carrie Judd Montgomery

The life of Carrie Judd Montgomery is a great example of one who cautiously approached the new signs and stirrings being released at Azusa Street at first, but then she pursued for more because she didn't want to miss out on what God had for her in her day. We have no idea what new signs will mark this next move of God. It will likely be weird and offensive to many and push us outside of our comfort zones. Carrie's story can inspire us not just to be open, but also to be hungry to take hold of all God has for us in our generation, regardless of what it might look like.

Carrie Judd Montgomery (1858-1946), one of the most influential women in the Divine Healing Movement in America, had already experienced the Spirit in a profound way previous to her own Pentecostal Spirit baptism experience.[67] As a young woman, she experienced a miraculous healing which empowered her for lifelong ministry. Before the heightened Holy Spirit stirrings in the early 1900s, she originally had thought that her first healing experience with the Spirit on February 26,1879 was her Spirit baptism. From that point on in her life, she had a very influential and pioneering healing ministry.

Carrie was in her late forties when the turn of the century came with the Azusa Street Revival in all its glory, making headlines. Even though she struggled and walked cautiously toward the things that were happening at the beginnings of this revival fire, she searched out this "Pentecostal baptism" for herself. Even with her profound ministry, she admitted that she "grew still more thirsty for the rivers of living water." She said that she knew she "had tiny streams, but not rivers."[68]

She proceeded to prayerfully seek God for the Spirit baptism experience that was gaining attention at the turn of the century. Her friend Lucy Simmons, who had already experienced her Spirit baptism, also encouraged her. It was with that same friend, on Monday June 29, 1908, that Carrie prayed for and received her Pentecostal baptism of the Holy Spirit. She was fifty years old at the time. Immediately following this overwhelming experience with the Spirit, Carrie spoke in tongues for nearly two hours.[69] She recorded her account below.

> For some time I have been thirsting for the fullness of the Holy Spirit's presence and power. At the time of my miraculous healing, when a young girl, I was first made conscious of the Holy Spirit's work in revealing Jesus in and to me. At this time a power to testify came into my soul, and the Word of God was wonderfully opened to me, so that He has greatly blessed my ministry in the Word since that time. This experience I have always referred to as the baptism of the Holy Ghost until a few months ago, when I began to watch what God was doing in pouring out His Pentecostal fullness upon some of His little ones. At first I was perplexed. I knew my experience, above referred to, was most real and lasting in its effects. How could I cast it away? Then I came to understand that I was not to depreciate His precious work in the past, but to follow on to receive the fullness of the same Spirit.[70]

Even though Carrie had already experienced the Holy Spirit's presence in her earlier healing encounter, she felt that there was still something more and she didn't want to miss out on what God had for her in her generation. She said, "I had myself received marvelous anointings of the Holy Spirit in the past, but I felt if there were more for me I surely wanted it, as I could not afford to miss any blessing that the Lord was pouring out in these last days."[71] When some of her friends received their

"Pentecost" experience and she noticed the transformations that took place in their lives, she began to hunger for something she never realized existed before.

It seems in the revivals of the early twentieth century, especially in the Azusa Street Revival, the Holy Spirit broke down barriers—even racial ones—to bring in a new outpouring of the Spirit that not many had been accustomed to before. While there were stories of Spirit baptisms with speaking in tongues scattered in history, Carrie most likely did not come across anyone who had received the baptism of the Holy Spirit with speaking of tongues until months before her own Spirit baptism experience. When Carrie saw deeper expressions of the Holy Spirit for the first time, she was awakened in her spirit to hunger for something she never realized was possible before that time. Simmons was one of the early people whom Carrie observed firsthand who had her Spirit baptism experience. Carrie admitted that she was somewhat skeptical of the "Pentecostal fullness" at first, but after seeing the positive effects it had on her friend, she was struck to the core enough to embrace the experience for herself.[72]

If Carrie, who was already thriving in her ministry, previously believed that she had already been baptized in the Holy Spirit, one must wonder what greater effect her "second" baptism of the Holy Spirit with the gift of tongues had on her life and her ministry. After this "second" Spirit baptism, Carrie claimed to have experienced a greater increase of joy, love, power for service, "teachableness," love of the Word of God, and "fellowship in prayer and praise."[73] She described in a sermon a few years after, that her "fuller baptism" experience resulted in "freedom of the mind from all care," which she had previously yet to settle.[74] She also described her life following her Spirit baptism as one where she mounted up with wings and gained physical strength in her body.

Carrie's baptism in the Holy Spirit also affected her ministry. Shortly after her experience, in her periodical called *Triumphs of Faith*, she became an advocate for the Pentecostal Spirit baptism while continuing to maintain a balanced view that love was the best result of Spirit baptism.[75] Additionally, instead of just collecting money for foreign missions, she went on an international ministry trip. It was during the trip that she was first used as a bridge between Evangelicals and Pentecostals to introduce this new experience and bring some clarity and understanding to missionaries on the field. While it is highly probable that Carrie would still have been effective in ministry if she continued in her present state without her Spirit baptism, she claimed that the experience added new dimensions to her ministry.

If Carrie Judd Montgomery, already a successful and effective leader in the Divine Healing Movement (she being only one of many in a similar situation), saw significance in this experience, then what does that say for successful ministers who have hesitated to explore Spirit baptism? What about Christians who believe this Spirit baptism experience is not for them because it's too "Pentecostal," are they missing out on anything? Carrie would most likely say yes to that question. While from her example, Spirit baptism might not transform one's whole ministry, Carrie did claim that it enhanced her ministry in new ways and added a depth to her spirituality. It also empowered her for her mission in a new way.

Whether it be Spirit baptism or a new move of God, Carrie's approach provides a great example for people from charismatic, Pentecostal, Evangelical, Baptist, and other traditions to follow. She was not just open, but she was also hungry to have all that the Spirit had to offer, even if it was not what she was used to. She believed that just because some people were fanatics in relation to this experience, this did not mean it was not from God or that it did not have value. She approached Spirit baptism with a cautious view, making sure not to throw out the "baby" with the bathwater.

Are we ready for revival even if it doesn't come the way we imagine? Most revivals were severely criticized before they became mainstream and accepted. Many times, the forerunners in one generation were the first to criticize and point fingers at those leading the next move. People didn't know how to handle something that looked different. Many people threw the "baby out with the bathwater," or failed to see the gold when other counterfeits emerged.

We can follow in Carrie's faith stream today in regards to approaching this next wave of the Spirit. The next time a strange phenomenon in relation to the work of the Spirit breaks out, hopefully we will be encouraged through Carrie's example not to miss out on all that the Spirit has for us just because it comes in a strange looking package. Nestled in with all that dirty bathwater, there might just be a precious baby who is waiting to be seen.

Regardless of how successful in ministry you already are, by learning from some early Pentecostals, specifically Carrie Judd Montgomery, there's a flooding and overwhelming experience of the Holy Spirit available for all who want to take hold of it. Like Carrie, will your hunger to encounter God lead you into more of His presence, no matter what it might look like in this generation?

I close with a blessing Carrie gave in 1910 from a sermon entitled, "Life on Wings: The Possibilities of Pentecost."

> Now, who is going to trust God for the winged life? You can crawl instead if you wish. God will even bless you if you crawl; He will do the best He can for you, but oh how much better to avail ourselves of our wonderful privileges in Christ and to "mount up with wings as eagles,

run and not be weary, walk and not faint." O beloved friends, there is a life on wings. I feel the streams of His life fill me and permeate my mortal frame from my head to my feet, until no words are adequate to describe it. I can only make a few bungling attempts to tell you what it is like and ask the Lord to reveal to you the rest. May He reveal to you your inheritance in Christ Jesus so that you will press on and get all that He has for you.[76]

5

THE FIRE SPREADS

THE POWER OF THE TESTIMONY

Once people had their Spirit baptism encounter, they would readily testify about this experience. The Azusa Mission often held testimony services that preceded the main service. Testimony after testimony also filled the pages of the Azusa Mission's periodical called *The Apostolic Faith*. Some of these stories were about people having their Pentecostal baptism of the Spirit, healings, the Shekinah glory "melting" people down at the meetings, or other God encounters. There was even a report sent into the *The Apostolic Faith* of someone being raised from the dead.[77] By reading the paper, many were able to draw from the testimonies and pray to have their own Pentecostal Spirit baptism encounter or receive healing. This newspaper was sent around the world for free to anyone who wanted it as God provided.[78] At its height, the periodical had over 50,000 subscribers. Many times, the articles were anonymous because they wanted God to get all of the glory.

MISSIONARIES LAUNCHED

There were many occasions when people got baptized in the Holy Spirit at the Mission and spoke in other known languages. Some of these people were sent into the nation of the language they spoke within days or soon after that happened, believing

God had called them and would provide the language while there.[79] In the early days at the Mission, they discovered that "the interpretation of the many messages in nearly every language spoken by the Holy Ghost in unknown tongues is that Jesus is coming."[80] Because early Pentecostals believed in premillennialism and that Jesus was coming back soon, missionaries were launched from the Azusa Mission at a rapid rate.[81] However, many of them realized upon arriving on the mission field that speaking in tongues was not sufficient to help them communicate in that land, and that they would need to learn the language.

While it may appear that they failed on the mission field, it is important to highlight that these zealous ones were open to take risks and experiment in discovering what God was doing in the world. Stepping out in faith to explore the mysteries of God is something to celebrate. If they never ventured to try something new, they may have never discovered the answer. One of the strengths of the early Pentecostals is that they weren't afraid to live outside the box, take risks, experiment, and explore new paths. This is one of the great attributes of this movement, and likely a quality that contributed to its rapid expansion.

By September 1906, evangelists who had received the fire at Azusa—meaning having been baptized by the Holy Ghost and spoke in tongues—went up and down the coast to spread that fire. This continued to spread to other cities across the United States. By December 1906, at least thirteen missionaries were sent from the Azusa Mission to Africa. By early 1907, missionaries were sent to Liberia, Mexico, Canada, Western Europe, the Middle East, West Africa, and Asia. By 1908, the movement had spread to South Africa, all across Europe, and into Russia.[82] One of the missionaries who was sent to Africa to carry the Pentecostal fire was Julia W. Hutchins, the same one who had kicked Seymour out of her church.[83] She eventually had her Spirit baptism encounter and was celebrated and even highlighted in *The Apostolic Faith*.[84] Love wins!

HOLY SPIRIT HOUSE FIRES

Soon after the flame was initially lit in the Bonnie Brae House, other house or "cottage" meetings began to emerge.[85] It was reported that in Los Angeles, "God has been setting homes on fire and coming down and melting and saving and sanctifying and baptizing with the Holy Ghost."[86] In the hills near Los Angeles,

> At a meeting recently held in a cottage near the church, one sister was baptized with the Holy Ghost on the front porch. She lay under the power of God for something like two hours, praising God and speaking in an unknown language. Two nights afterward, at another cottage prayer meeting, the house was filled to overflowing with people. The meeting lasted until one o'clock in the morning. Five were baptized with the Holy Ghost and three were sanctified. Two sisters lay under the power of God until after one o'clock, speaking and singing in unknown tongues. The singing could be heard over the hills. This is stirring the people, and God is going to work wonders in this place.[87]

Other times, while saints gathered to worship God in cottage meetings, people passing by would receive an overflow of God's glory manifesting in that environment. One blind man walked by a cottage meeting and got convicted when he overheard people praying in tongues. As a result, he got saved and had his sight restored.[88] Still other times, "the fire" would fall on people and they would pray and sing in tongues for hours, receive visions from heaven, or be slain in the Spirit while attending cottage prayer meetings.[89]

Sometimes cottage meetings broke out because local churches rejected the new Pentecostal Spirit baptism, so people had to gather together in homes to pray for this. Other times, people gathered together in homes because God apprehended them before they could leave for the meeting.[90] One time, a few people were on their way to an evening service when they stopped by someone's house to have a time of prayer first. The presence of God crashed in with such power that they were unable to continue to the meeting, several speaking and singing in tongues.[91] There were other times where people couldn't even eat because the presence of God was so powerful.

> One morning in the cottage on the Mission grounds, two were healed before breakfast. Another morning at the family worship two were slain under the power and one received the baptism with the Holy Ghost. The dining room is a blessed place. The power comes down so upon the workers that we can scarcely eat. We sing, speak in tongues and praise God at the table. The food from heaven is the best part of the meal.[92]

Spiritual house fires were ignited around the city and in other nations as people were hungry to encounter God in a greater measure no matter what it looked like. Even in Australia there were cottage meetings where God's incoming presence marked the people and many received their personal Pentecost.[93] During the Azusa Street Revival, God apprehended people both in church meetings and at homes. People gathered together at the Mission or in intimate spaces for one purpose: to encounter God like never before.

While the Welsh Revival was marked by mass salvations and social transformation, the Azusa Street Revival was marked by the Pentecostal Spirit baptism encounter. They believed that this experience would embolden them with greater power to take the gospel to the ends of the earth. When these Spirit-baptized saints spread the Pentecostal message through testimonies and impartation, others would also be led to have their Spirit baptism and be empowered to step into their callings. *The Apostolic Faith* newspaper mailed reports and testimonies around the world, spreading the revival fire on a more global scale. Missionaries were also sent out from Azusa carrying the fire and introducing many to the new Spirit baptism encounter. As a result of these Christians being set on fire for Jesus, societies and nations would eventually be transformed.

6

THE FIRE
BURNS DEEP

As the fire began to spread around the world, it also began to burn deep in people. In addition to the empowering encounter of Spirit baptism at the heart of the revival, living in purity, holiness, and total consecration was also emphasized at the Mission. Inviting the fire of God to come and burn away anything contrary to God's nature manifested as a feeling of God "melting" people down under His incoming presence. Fire brought a deep consecration to the people.

TOTAL CONSECRATION

Total consecration was a mark of this revival. Seymour wanted people to be sanctified before he would pray for them to receive their Pentecostal Spirit baptism. He wanted the people to be pure and clean vessels before they were filled with power from on high. Consecration is when one wholly yields to the leading of the Holy Spirit no matter the cost. It is an unreserved yes to whatever God calls us to do. It is being willing to walk in holiness and purity and being set apart from the ways of the world to be wholly devoted to Jesus. When God has one person fully yielded who will say yes to anything He asks, He can change a nation through that one. It's happened before and it will continue to be available to us today. Bartleman said it well:

All believers are called to a one hundred per cent consecration. God has no two standards of consecration for the foreign missionary, and the home Christian. We cannot find it in the Bible. One is called to consecrate their all as well as the other, as God's steward, in their own place and calling. One goes, one prays, and one gives. It takes the three to make a missionary.[94]

The sacred and the secular cannot be divided or separated. God has to be able to permeate us wherever He plants us in each season.

The early leaders at Azusa burned for righteous living and the sanctified life. One of the leaders at the Mission said,

The Lord wants a people in these days that will make the very highest consecration to God. He wants us to step up to the heights of holiness. We are at a time when we ought to be looking for the greatest revival the world has ever had.[95]

Total surrender precedes many, though not all, personal and corporate moves of God, awakenings, and outpourings of the Holy Spirit. It is also a common result of what happens after one has had a profound encounter with God. Surrender allows God to come and fill and fully possess one with the Holy Spirit without anything getting in the way.

What does it look like to live a consecrated life where God has placed us? What does it look like to give a complete yes to the One who gave everything for us? Ask God which areas in your life you need to surrender to Him. Dare to pursue greater holiness. Ask the Holy Spirit to purify and sanctify those areas in your life that need to be refined by His fire. Invite the Holy Spirit to consecrate and set you apart in a deeper way today.

MELTING UNDER THE FIRE OF GOD

The fire of God was a prominent theme at Azusa. God "melted" people down with His incoming presence. People burned with passion for Jesus. There are even reports of people claiming to see fire "issuing" from the Mission itself. One young boy "saw a ball of fire in the top of the tabernacle which broke and filled the whole place with light."[96]

The flame of God at the Mission searched people's hearts. In the midst of demons being cast out, the sick healed, many saved, restored, and baptized in power, Bartleman noted,

> Heroes are being developed, the weak made strong in the Lord. Men's hearts are being searched as with a lighted candle. It is a tremendous sifting time, not only of actions, but of inner, secret motives. Nothing can escape the all-searching eye of God. Jesus is being lifted up, the "blood" magnified, and the Holy Spirit honored once more.[97]

As people got closer to the fire of God, everything that opposed His nature melted away, hearts were softened, and lives purified.[98]

When describing God's incoming presence in the early days at Azusa, many referred to being "melted" by the power of God. One man received his Pentecost and claimed to be "filled and saturated with the melting power of God."[99] Pride, sin, and fear dissipated as love emerged. Melting under the power of God also caused the people to be united together, regardless of race.

> This meeting has been a melting time. The people are all melted together by the power of the blood and the Holy Ghost. They are made one lump, one bread, all one body in Christ Jesus. There is no Jew or Gentile, bond or free, in the Azusa Street Mission.[100]

They were made one in Christ Jesus as they were melted together by His incoming presence.

What does it look like to be melted together under the fire of God? The Azusa Street story teaches us the importance of sanctification and holiness. When we ask for the fire to come, are we ready to let go of everything that opposes His nature? Are we willing for all the excess in our lives to be burned up and stripped away so that only what remains is pure gold?

God is truly raising up burning ones in our day. Burning ones are formed in the fire. These refined ones become unstoppable because the hidden recesses of the heart have already been penetrated by the fire and love of God. One of the authors of *The Apostolic Faith* wrote,

> God's ministers are "a flame of fire." He wants men and women all on fire. He wants us not only saved from sin but on fire. The Holy Ghost is dynamite and fire in your soul.[101]

Ask for the fire of God to fall upon and fill you today like never before.

BAPTISM OF FIRE

While Azusa Street was marked primarily with a baptism of the Holy Spirit and a baptism of fire, I declare that the next move of God will be marked with an even greater baptism of fire and of love than what they experienced. In Matthew 3:11, John the Baptist said,

> I baptize you with water for repentance. But after me will come one who is more powerful than I, whose sandals I am not fit to carry. He will baptize you with the Holy Spirit and with fire.

Fire purifies, refines, sanctifies, makes holy, and brings a burning. It causes all the dross to dissipate and only the gold to emerge. Asking for the baptism of fire strips off any enemy of the cross of Christ, even good things that are distractions. There's no greater way to be surrendered than when we are willing to ask God to send His fire over every detail of our lives, relationships, dreams, and thoughts, and ask Him to burn away anything that is not from Him for this season. When we realize the price He has paid for us (see Romans 8:32), we will be willing to become living sacrifices (see Romans 12:1) and we will continue to lay our lives on the altar to burn for Him daily. In Leviticus 6:12-13, it says

> The fire on the altar must be kept burning; it must not go out. Every morning the priest is to add firewood and arrange the burnt offering on the fire and burn the fat of the fellowship offerings on it. The fire must be kept burning on the altar continuously; it must not go out.

What would happen if we lived in a baptism of fire daily? What does it look like to be a burning one in this generation and to not burn out? What does it look like to be a living sacrifice where God's all-consuming fire invades our lives daily?

There is more for each one of us today. God is asking us to call out for the fire of God to come and consume anything that might get in the way of all He wants to do in our lives. I encourage you right now to ask for the fire of God to fall upon you and for this fire to burn away any bitterness, unforgiveness, double-mindedness, offense, fear, shame, insecurity, disappointment, hopelessness, or discouragement. Ask God to search your heart to see if there is anything holding you back from all that He has. Now, wait on Him for a few minutes.

As the Holy Spirit brings up people and situations, go and be reconciled today. Don't delay. If someone has an offense against you, go and make amends quickly. Give no foothold to the devil in this time of great awakening. Always remember that our battle is never against flesh and blood (see Ephesians 6:10-18) and that you have authority in Christ to tear down every stronghold or enemy of God that tries to oppose you (see Romans 8:31).

Stay deeply connected and knit together with the body of Christ in this season, for they will also be your armor bearers. When the fire falls, the pruning begins, and you feel the pain of things leaving in your life that you were once comfortable with, ask for even more fire. He wants to purify us so we are prepared to carry what He is about to pour out across the earth. He is looking for pure and holy vessels that He can possess and fill with His Holy Spirit, His glory, and His fire. I encourage you to pray the following prayer out loud.

God, I ask right now to be marked by a burning passion and love for Jesus like never before. I ask for a fresh baptism of fire over my life today. Let Your fire fall on every single detail of my life. Burn away anything and everything that is not in line with You in Jesus' name. Purify with fire all of my relationships, thoughts, dreams, desires, and situations. Burn away anything that is contrary to Your nature or that will hold me back from all that You want to do in and through my life in this season. I surrender all and ask for the fire of consecration to come and set me apart as a burning one for You. Let my love for You be marked by purity, holiness, and a burning passion. Fill and possess me with Your Holy Spirit and with fire. Let my heart burn for You like never before. Reignite the fire inside. I am all Yours. My life is in Your hands. Have Your way in me today, whatever it looks like and no matter the cost. I live only for Your glory. In Jesus' name I pray, Amen.

7

FLOWING WITH
THE HOLY SPIRIT

LEADERSHIP AT AZUSA

The early participants at Azusa sought to give the Holy Spirit total freedom in leading the meetings and the movement. William J. Seymour led the Mission open-handed, giving space to the Holy Spirit to move through anyone in the room. When Seymour did rise to partner with what the Holy Spirit was doing, he did it humbly. Bartleman noticed that Seymour "generally sat behind two empty shoe boxes, one on top of the other. He usually kept his head inside the top one during the meeting, in prayer. There was no pride there."[102] He further recounted,

> Brother Seymour was recognized as the nominal leader in charge. But we had no pope or hierarchy. We were "brethren." We had no human programme. The Lord Himself was leading. We had no priest class, nor priest craft...We did not even have a platform or pulpit in the beginning. All were on a level.[103]

After Seymour got married on May 13, 1908 to Jennie Evans Moore, they made their home in a small apartment in the upper floor of the Mission.[104] Several of the workers lived in apartments upstairs at the Mission as well. They were living in community right in the heartbeat of the revival. There was also a room upstairs where people would go to pray for and receive their personal Pentecost and another room to pray for healing.[105]

When the leadership at Azusa didn't see God move as much as they had hoped, they went to prayer and fasting, entreating God "for more power in the meetings." One time in response to their cries, they "felt an increase of power every night."[106] God crashed in and many were slain in the Spirit and marked by God, while others "came through" and were baptized in the Holy Spirit.

THE COLOR LINE WAS
WASHED AWAY IN THE BLOOD

Seymour "provided the vision of a truly color-blind congregation" during a time of racial segregation, says Azusa Street historian Cecil M. Robeck, Jr.[107] One of the biggest breakthroughs at Azusa Street was that the walls of race and gender were broken down. Bartleman observed that "the 'color line' was washed away in the blood."[108] This was in relation to racial divides being abolished by the blood of Jesus. To have people from different races worshipping alongside one another and praying for each other during a time when lynchings were common and many years before Martin Luther King, Jr. came onto the scene is truly

William J. Seymour and his team. Standing from left to right are Phoebe Sargent, G.W. Evans, Jennie Evans Moore, Glenn A. Cook, Florence Louise Crawford, Thomas Junk, and Sister Prince. Seated from left to right are May Evans, Hiram W. Smith with Mildred Crawford sitting on his lap, William J. Seymour, and Clara Lum.

remarkable.[109] In fact, it was when Seymour was praying along-side a white man until the early hours of the morning that he first spoke in tongues.

Seymour's early leadership team was racially mixed and included women. Giving women room to testify and to have a voice was also radical in that era. Regular participants of the Mission in the early years included people from various ethnicities and backgrounds including African-Americans, European Americans, Hispanic Americans, Asian Americans, Native Americans, and more.[110] Visitors would come to Azusa and experience such love and humility present in the people. One person said, "From the first time I entered I was struck by the blessed spirit that prevailed in the meeting, such a feeling of unity and humility among the children of God."[111]

The early days of the Azusa Street Revival were marked by unity, humility, and love. Seymour emphasized the need to develop the fruit of the Spirit, especially love. While there was great emphasis on speaking in tongues as a sign or initial evidence of Spirit baptism in the earliest stages of the revival, by the summer of 1907—possibly because of the overemphasis of speaking in tongues—likely Seymour himself wrote the following instructions to the "baptized saints,"

> Tongues are one of the signs that go with every baptized person, but it is not the real evidence of the baptism in the every day life. Your life must measure with the fruits of the Spirit. If you get angry, or speak evil, or backbite, I care not how many tongues you may have, you have not the baptism with the Holy Spirit.[112]

In 1908, the leadership at Azusa said, "The Pentecostal power, when you sum it all up, is just more of God's love."[113] In response to the question about what the real evidence is that a person has received the baptism of the Holy Ghost, they answered, "Divine love, which is charity."[114] Love was what was needed for this baptism of the Holy Spirit experience to be sustainable. What will happen in our day when love supersedes theological debates and differences among our brothers and sisters in Christ?

SPONTANEOUS

When people went to a meeting at Azusa, they had no idea what to expect or what the meeting might look like. The meetings began on their own, "spontaneously, in testimony, praise and worship." Sometimes there would be a handful of people "trembling under the mighty power of God" during a meeting. It was God who initiated this, not a speaker. God was "liable to burst through any one" during a meeting and that was welcomed whether it be through a child, man, or woman, regardless of race.[115]

Billboards or social media campaigns were not used to announce a special speaker of the hour. They did not promote or advertise who would be on the platform but rather invited people to come and encounter God together. The people were hungry to hear from God no matter who He spoke through.[116]

Those at Azusa made room for the Holy Spirit to lead in the meetings through whomever the anointing was on at that time. Anointing is when the Holy Spirit inspires someone to release a message, word, dance, song, or other act in unison with what God is doing or wanting to release at a particular time.[117] The leadership at Azusa encouraged those who had received their personal Pentecost to remain in the anointing.

> The Lord wants everything that is done in a meeting to be done in the anointing of the Holy Ghost. The Holy Ghost comes into your body for service. He anoints His ministers afresh for every service. Every song and every testimony should be given under the anointing of the Holy Ghost. Some have learned how to preach but it is a good

thing for you if you cannot speak without the anointing of the Holy Ghost. You can get down on your knees and ask the Lord to use you or to set you aside, which ever He wills, and to put the anointing on you for service if He wants to give you a message. Pretty soon you will feel the power going all over you. All you need to do is to yield to the will of God.[118]

What does it look like to fully yield to the Spirit and to steward the anointing today, even if it comes from an unlikely source?[119]

OUR TIME WAS THE LORD'S

A mark of many revivals is that time is irrelevant when God shows up. It becomes normal for people to get apprehended or slain in the Spirit for hours, sometimes even days. Nobody wants to leave the manifest presence of God. People will miss school or work because they want God more than anything. At Azusa, it was no different. Bartleman noted, "We had no prear-ranged programme to be jammed through on time. Our time was the Lord's."[120] They had trouble closing at night because of the seekers still present and those who were "under the power of God."[121] Bartleman said that

> The services ran almost continuously. Seeking souls could be found under the power almost any hour, night and day. The place was never closed nor empty. The people came to meet God. He was always there. Hence a continuous meeting. The meeting did not depend on the human leader. God's presence became more and more wonderful.[122]

Bartleman noticed that people were out "under the power all night" at times. He also saw that

> There was no closing at 9 o'clock sharp, as the preachers must do today in order to keep the people. We wanted God in those days. We did not have a thousand other things we wanted before Him.[123]

Wow, what a profound statement! What does it look like to "not have a thousand other things" we want before God? What will happen when knowing Jesus becomes the sole purpose of our lives each day? May we become possessed once again by the Holy Spirit and may Jesus remain the most important focus of our lives today and every day.

SHEKINAH GLORY

Another mark of this revival is the Shekinah glory. The manifest presence of God was so thick and powerful in the meetings that people could sense His presence blocks away. Bartleman noticed

> The shekinah glory rested there. In fact some claim to have seen the glory by night over the building. I do not doubt it. I have stopped more than once within two blocks of the place and prayed for strength before I dared go on. The presence of the Lord was so real.[124]

> In the early "Azusa" days both Heaven and hell seemed to have come to town. Men were at the breaking point. Conviction was mightily on the people. They would fly to pieces even on the street, almost without provocation. A very "dead line" seemed to be drawn around "Azusa Mission," by the Spirit. When men came within two or three blocks of the place they were seized with conviction.[125]

Some even saw the Shekinah glory resting "as a pillar of fire by night" upon the building.[126] In the glory, there was no need for man to help people get to God. When the Spirit fell upon the congregation in a meeting, people ran to the front for salvation. Others got slain in the Spirit and encountered God for hours. The early participants at Azusa sought to host God's presence well within their community so much so that the glory became manifested in the physical.

What does it look like to be so full of God's glory that our faces shine like Moses' face when he came down from the mountain after forty days with God? What does it look like to host, steward, and invite the glory of God to fill our lives, communities, and times together so much that people walking by get apprehended and recognize that God is present?

THE SLAIN OF THE LORD

In the midst of the Azusa Street Revival, many people were slain in the Spirit. They would fall out in the Spirit only to rise speaking in new tongues and fully transformed.[127] Numerous ones had powerful encounters with God while they were out in the Spirit. When God apprehended them, they yielded.[128] In August 1906, Bartleman noted that there was much "slaying power" manifested in the meetings and that "strong men lie for hours under the mighty power of God, cut down like grass."[129] Even the preachers would fall on their faces during the meetings because they were so "taken up with God." Bartleman claimed it "was almost impossible to stay off our faces in those days. The presence of the Lord was so real." He even said that they almost felt like apologizing for taking people's attention off of God to make announcements, not wanting to touch or interfere with what God was doing in the meeting.[130]

When God apprehends us, will we yield to His leading, even if that looks like being on the floor for hours or even days?

HEALING

Healing for the sick was also prevalent in the meetings at Azusa. The walls were covered with the crutches and canes that got left behind after people were healed. The Mission had a prayer room upstairs to pray for the sick. It was almost a daily occurrence for people to be healed from various issues including cancer, rheumatism, paralysis, consumption (now called tuberculosis), and many other sicknesses.[131] Relational healing and reconciliation were also prevalent in the revival:

> The people have been paying up old debts, making wrongs right, getting hard feelings out of the way, etc. One who was saved from drink confessed to crimes and offered to pay the penalty of the law. People living in adultery or where one party had a living husband or wife have separated, and God is wonderfully pouring out His Spirit on this line of things.[132]

Those at the Azusa Mission also had prayer meetings for requests mailed in from around the world where they saw wonderful answers to prayer.[133] When people got healed, the leaders at Azusa stewarded these testimonies by creating space for them to be shared in a service or by releasing these stories in writing. Though healing was prominent in the meetings, it was never the focus of this revival like Spirit baptism was.

MUSIC OF THE REVIVAL

Music marks every revival and new move of God. Worship music shapes the theology of culture and of generations. What people sing becomes a declaration of their heart's cry and what they truly believe. Singing in the Spirit in other tongues was a regular occurrence in the Azusa meetings. Bartleman gave a snapshot of what worship was like in the early days of the revival.

> In the beginning in "Azusa" we had no musical instruments. In fact we felt no need of them. There was no place for them in our worship. All was spontaneous. We did not even sing from hymn books. All the old, well known hymns were sung from memory, quickened by the Spirit of God. "The Comforter Has Come," was possibly the one most sung. We sang it from fresh, powerful heart experience. Oh, how the power of God filled and thrilled us. Then the "blood" songs were very popular. "The life is in the blood," Sinai, Calvary, and Pentecost, all

had their rightful place in the "Azusa" work. But the "new song" was altogether different, not of human composition. It cannot be successfully counterfeited.[134]

What kind of new songs and sounds will emerge in our generation? What would it look like to merge and integrate revival songs from the past into new sounds today with a fresh feel? In the arena of music, is there a way to access and tap into the power of the testimony by integrating pieces of what God breathed on past generations with what He is doing today?

The Azusa Street Revival was free flowing with new sounds and with plenty of room for the Holy Spirit to come and move spontaneously through whomever was anointed in that moment. People came to the Mission and never knew what to expect. They came hungry for more of God and didn't want to leave until He touched them deeply. The continuous meetings at the Mission with its late hours gave people permission to be marked by God without a time limit of when they would have to leave. It didn't matter what race a person was, they were all one in the Lord. In their unity, the Shekinah glory of the Lord rested in a powerful way. What greater signs, wonders, miracles, and glory might we experience when the church unites under the blood of Jesus to love each other and seek after God with everything within us?

8

SEYMOUR'S LIFE
AFTER THE REVIVAL

For three years from 1906-1909, the Azusa Street Mission hosted daily meetings around the clock.[135] Revival broke out, impacting nations. And while the revival fire spread rapidly around the world, it eventually waned in Los Angeles and was met with challenges. Because of the great glory present at the Mission and the freedom Seymour gave to the leading of the Holy Spirit, leaders were drawn to the anointing and wanted to take over. Seymour and the Mission experienced opposition time and time again.

Some of the opposition to the Mission came from the outside. God was moving in great and unusual ways at Azusa and many did not like that. The secular newspapers wrote negative reports, but that only helped provide free advertising for what God was doing. However, the hardest part of dealing with the opposition for Seymour was when it came from his friends. In October of 1906, Seymour's mentor, Charles Parham, visited the Mission in response to his invitation. Parham didn't like what he saw and he began to criticize the work, eventually trying to assume leadership. When Seymour's congregation would not yield, Parham set up his own meetings nearby. Seymour was disillusioned by what happened from this once friend and mentor.

Not long after Seymour's marriage to Jennie in May 1908, Clara Lum, the editor helping with *The Apostolic Faith*, left for Portland, Oregon taking with her all of the mailing addresses for the paper. She joined Florence Crawford in her mission there and continued to print *The Apostolic Faith* from there, redirecting those on the mailing list at that time to send donations to Portland instead of to Los Angeles. Seymour failed to recover the addresses and his mission suffered the loss.

Seymour continued to travel and evangelize in spite of the challenges he faced. While he was traveling in 1911, his wife decided to invite William H. Durham to preach at the Mission. During his time there, Durham tried to gain control of the Mission. Seymour came home early to Durham's surprise. Seymour consulted his board and they decided to lock the doors of the church so Durham could no longer minister, and thus he regained control of the Mission. Durham went to another mission a few blocks away to continue building his ministry.[136]

By 1915, Seymour's congregation continued to dwindle. Because of all the hardship he had encountered with white people who used to be mentors, friends, or leaders in his life, he succumbed to making sure that his main leadership team was all African-American. One of the strengths of the early Azusa revival was that there was unity between the races. Unfortunately, through hardship and betrayal, this wonderful characteristic of the revival dissolved.

On September 28, 1922, Seymour breathed his last breath after a heart attack. His wife continued on in the ministry, still having to try to ward people off who were trying to take control of the Mission. She continued to pastor there until 1931, when the church was torn down because no parties were able to buy it and steward its historical legacy. Jennie and a small group of remaining church attendees returned to meet in the Asberry home on Bonnie Brae Street where the revival was originally ignited. What began in the context of seeking God together in a home, and then spread throughout the world before it died down in Los Angeles, ended in that same home for Jennie and some of the original few.

Seymour ended his days with a dwindled congregation, with racism still prevalent in his surrounding area, and rejected by those he tried to minister to over the years, all the while becoming a significant catalyst of a worldwide revival that is still impacting people today. While it can be somewhat disillusioning to hear that the catalytic leader of this revival died in relative obscurity and pain, the momentum he helped set in motion continues to have an increasing impact for the kingdom of God over one hundred years later.

One person saying yes to Jesus and not giving up can create a momentum so great in his or her lifetime that it can impact nations and generations to come. Though the revival was short-lived in Los Angeles, the well they dug during that time was deeper than anyone could ever imagine.

THE FLAMES INCREASE

The Azusa Street Revival was catalytic for the growth, expansion, and development of the Pentecostalism movement.[137] Pentecostalism spread when people visited the Azusa Mission, had their personal Pentecost experience and spoke in tongues, and then left to integrate this new experience into their theology and practice. A few of the leaders who received their Spirit baptism at Azusa were G.B. Cashwell,[138] C.H. Mason (the founder of The Church of God in Christ), William H. Durham, Mary Rumsey (who ministered in Korea), A.H. Argue (who became a Pentecostal leader in Canada), John G. Lake, and countless others.[139]

The Azusa Street Mission

The Anglican vicar from England, Alexander A. Boddy, visited Azusa and went back home, integrating the Pentecostal message into his Anglican church. It was through his ministry that healing evangelist Smith Wigglesworth eventually had his Pentecostal Spirit baptism experience. Wigglesworth was ready to return home from Boddy's Sunderland meetings without speaking in tongues, but when he went to say goodbye to Boddy's wife, Mary, he asked for prayer once more. She laid hands on him and he had a powerful Spirit baptism encounter and spoke in tongues for the first time.

Carrie Judd Montgomery spoke in tongues in 1908 and as a result spread the Pentecostal message around the world through her missionary tour and her periodical *Triumphs of Faith*. She was used as a bridge to introduce many significant evangelical leaders to the new experience. Many more were indirectly influenced by Azusa when they encountered a Spirit-baptized person and received impartation for the same thing. A pastor named Owen Adams from Monrovia, California had his Spirit baptism encounter at Azusa and spoke in tongues. He later shared his testimony with Robert Semple, who eventually had his Pentecostal Spirit baptism in Chicago under Durham's ministry. Aimee Kennedy attended a meeting led by Robert Semple who preached this message of Pentecostal fullness. His message stirred her hunger for more, which eventually led to her having her Spirit baptism encounter and speaking in tongues. These two eventually married. Aimee Semple McPherson later went on to found what is now called the International Church of the Foursquare Gospel in Los Angeles.[140]

A few more of the denominations that have been birthed or influenced directly or indirectly by Azusa Street are the Church of God (Cleveland, Tennessee), the Church of God in Christ (COGIC), the Pentecostal Holiness church, Assemblies of God, Pentecostal Church of God, the Elim Movement, and many more. Demos Shakarian, who founded the Full Gospel Businessmen's Fellowship, claimed that his grandfather was an early Azusa Street Revival participant.[141]

There are over six hundred million Pentecostals and charismatics today in almost every nation of the world in what is known as one of the fastest-growing religious movements in history.[142] Charismatics are those who had existing structures or denominations for worship but decided to integrate some of the Pentecostal distinctives into their already-established congregations like Boddy and many others did. Many more traditional Protestant churches, as well as several streams within the Catholic Church, have also embraced the Pentecostal message. Historian Vinson Synan says, "Few events have affected modern church history as greatly as the famous Azusa Street revival of 1906-1909 which ushered into being the worldwide twentieth-century Pentecostal renewal."[143] While what remains in Los Angeles from the Azusa Street Revival today might not seem significant, the global impact this revival had and continues to have around the world surpasses what anyone would have originally dreamed.

The Azusa Street Mission became an apostolic center that ignited people with a fire that continues to burn and spread today. Pentecostalism is still the fastest-growing form of Christianity. The great number of divisions within Pentecostal churches over theological issues has actually played a part in spreading and multiplying the Pentecostal message to more people. It is believed that more people have been saved in connection with this revival and its influences than from many past centuries accumulated. What was released and birthed out of Azusa has impacted and continues to impact the world today.[144]

This all started when one man said yes to God and would not give up on all that God had for him in his generation until he broke through. He even taught about Spirit baptism before he had experienced it because he knew it was available by clinging to the testimonies and teachings of the forerunners who had gone before him. Social, racial, and gender barriers were broken because of the single-minded purpose to simply encounter God no matter what it looked like. Even if it was embarrassing, criticized, or said to be the work of Satan, the early Azusa saints didn't budge from breaking a generation into more of what God had for them in their day. They pressed on until they broke through.

These saints at Azusa were forerunners who ushered in a new era for their generation. A handful of friends wanting to encounter God in a greater measure and not giving up until they "came through," birthed a movement that is continuing to have ripple effects even today. Think of what transformation might result today when the desire found in early Pentecostal prayer circles at the Bonnie Brae House and Azusa Street Mission, marked by an intense hunger to be overwhelmed and to be baptized in the Spirit, becomes a renewed prayer for us today. What will it look like when a new generation of hungry ones follow in the Azusa saints' footsteps and seek together for a greater outpouring of the Spirit than ever before? What will happen when we persist and pursue Him until He comes in a greater measure? Might we see a new Jesus Revolution today?

We have dug deep into this well of revival at Azusa. Much has been pioneered on our behalf. We can now take what these saints of old have fought for and build upon it. Now it's our turn to ride on the momentum they created so we can go even further and pave the way for future generations. Azusa was not just a revival that happened over one hundred years ago, it is a testimony of God's story, filled with keys that will unlock hidden treasures and propel us into a greater future.

PART TWO

9

PREPARING TO STEWARD THE NEXT GREAT AWAKENING

MOMENTUM

While those at Azusa sought to restore what was lost in the early church in the book of Acts, this next move of God will be marked by synergy and momentum.[145] Just as a tidal wave gets bigger the closer it gets to land, this next move of God builds upon the momentum of centuries past. Rather than only pulling from the early church of Acts, we are also building on the momentum of Martin Luther and the Reformation, John Wesley and the Great Awakening, Charles Finney, the Divine Healing Movement, the Welsh Revival, Azusa Street Revival, and many more. We are not just building on one of these revivals; we are riding on the accumulated momentum of them all. There is great synergy here that will propel us into a greater dimension of God's glory than in times past.[146] As we step into what God has for us in our generation, it will also be important to position ourselves and to steward this revival well.

CREATING A CULTURE TO STEWARD
THE BILLION-SOUL HARVEST

Today, we have been given an incredible opportunity to create a new normal for what this next generation and beyond can be. Imagine what future generations will look like if those from this incoming billion-soul harvest get born into a family of burning Jesus lovers who are marked by intimacy, signs, wonders, love, and family. Whatever culture we welcome the flood of new believers into will become their normal. That's why one of the questions we need to ask is, what kind of culture do we want these new believers to be born into?

Many of us have spent years building our relationship with Christ. We have invested countless hours worshipping at Jesus' feet and simply being with Him. We have grown in prayer, fasting, and reading the Word. We have invested time, energy, and even resources to learn how to prophesy, grow in greater faith to step out to heal the sick, and to follow the leading of the Spirit at all costs. But what if when the new harvest comes, our ceiling becomes their floor? What if prayer, fasting, and reading the Word become their starting point and new normal? What if they get born into a culture marked by intimacy with Jesus and family? What will happen if this billion-soul harvest gets invited into a family of believers who do life centered on the presence of God and who also do great exploits for the kingdom together? What does it look like to have someone born into a culture that stewards intimacy with Jesus and is committed to the body of Christ in love? We have the opportunity to shape what the next era of Christianity will look like and to create a new wineskin for the new wine that's about to be poured out.

One of the major challenges in the Welsh Revival, when thousands got saved all at once, was that there was little discipleship. The new converts had a profound experience with God, but then because they had no one to disciple them, some of them became knee-deep—or shallow—Christians. Many of them never got rooted in God's Word and in community. Rees Howells (1879-1950), an intercessor and participant in the Welsh Revival, recognized that when the multitudes started coming to know the Lord, there was a massive need for discipleship for the revival to be sustainable.

> But the real problem arose as the Revival proceeded and thousands were added to the churches. There were more children born than there were nurses to tend to them. The establishing of converts became the greatest need, which if not met would be the most dangerous weakness of the Revival...As enthusiasm abated, there were bound to be many who had depended more on feelings and not yet learned to have their faith solidly based on the Word of God.[147]

Today, you have a longer history with Jesus than someone who is about to be born into the kingdom of God. Regardless of how qualified you feel or not, there is a great responsibility to disciple these new Christians with the Word of God and to help them grow deep in their relationship with Jesus and with community. Right now you might not feel like much of a leader. You might be one person in a sea of many other leaders. Very soon the tide is going to change. The hidden and silent Christians will soon become leaders of many. Be prepared to disciple and to give away what God has given you, wherever you are at in your journey. These soon-to-be-born baby Christians will need mothers and fathers, and big sisters and brothers to help them find their way. God has anointed and appointed you for such a time as this. When He positions you in a place where you feel overwhelmed because you are leading more than you feel capable of, simply lean upon Him. It's not by your power or might that you will be able to accomplish anything for Him. It is by His Spirit that you will be able to stand and fulfill the call of God on your life in this generation (Zechariah 4:6).

FAMILY: THE FIREPLACE FOR REVIVAL

One of the greatest movements in history that contributed to the rapid spread of Christianity began when God crashed in on a handful of family and friends who were hungry for more of God. The Azusa Street Revival actually began as the "Bonnie Brae Street Revival" before it contributed to the spread of global Pentecostalism. The fruit that was released from this little tribe who gathered together in a home on Bonnie Brae Street is incredible.[148] There is something significant about seeking God together with friends and inviting Him to invade even the intimate spaces of family.

Revival begins and is sustained in family. In this next era, Christianity will burst from the seams of churches, communities, homes, families, and intimate spaces and be carried over into the world. The Sunday morning worship celebrations will be important to testify and share more widely about what God is doing in the city, the region, and the world. The place of intimacy and connection will also need to be cultivated in smaller communities as more people enter into the family of God.

Being intentional with community will be an important factor in stewarding this next move of God like it was for those at Azusa. Doing life together with a small tribe of our people will be an important aspect of stewarding and discipling this incoming harvest. Staying known in a close-knit community with others who burn for Jesus is a key for sustaining revival and finishing well. Evan Roberts isolated himself many times from community, and the revival died down shortly after. Healing evangelist Kathryn Kuhlman got herself into some marital trouble when she wouldn't listen to her friends. Cultivating healthy community is important for continuing to burn—and to not burn out.

In the wild, no matter how strong a zebra is, if it is away from the pack when the lions come, it gets picked off and killed. It's not the weakest that fall; it's the ones who stray from their tribe. We need each other to fulfill our truest destiny. We can't do it alone. There are keys to our destiny that are hidden within the lives and hearts of those whom God has positioned us to run with in each season. The way to access these keys in each other is to intentionally do life together, be vulnerable, love each other well, and go after the things of God together.

As we begin to go after praying for stadiums full of people being saved, at the same time, we need to realize the importance of going deeper with the few. We can only go deep with a handful of people at one time. Jesus had the twelve, but then He also had Peter, James, and John, with John as His most intimate friend. They lived together, traveled together, ate together, ministered together, and did life together.

There is something important about doing life together in God's presence. Close community was crucial to the beginnings of the Azusa Street Revival just as it was for Jesus in His ministry. Homes represent intimate spaces of family and deep friendships. It's easy to blend in with the crowd in larger settings and slip out without really letting anyone in. People can't hide or avoid the deeper things of the heart in a home or small community.

The keys to our destiny are found in family and in intimacy with Jesus. Examples in history of this include the Moravian community in Herrnhut, Germany which started the 24/7 prayer movement and also those in the Jesus People Movement who opened community houses for the new believers. Family hosts the fire of God in a greater way than an individual can do alone.

I wonder what it would look like to invite God into the home in a greater measure today. What does it look like to cultivate a burning fire within the context of family? And what might be the potential effects for the world when that happens? What does it look like in our ministries or churches to become family, to do life together, to be present in intimate places and spaces with people? How can we cultivate that in this season? I encourage you to ask God to highlight a few people in your life right now who you can pursue deeper connection with. Then, I challenge you this week to take a risk, be bold and courageous, and pursue deeper connection and vulnerability with at least one person highlighted to you. Watch and see what God wants to do in your midst in and through your community.

As your fire for Jesus burns even brighter, I pray that you would burn with other burning ones and that God would place you in family and in covenant relationships so that you are known, loved, championed, and never alone.

10

INTIMACY: THE KEY TO KEEPING THE FLAME

by Heidi Baker

Heidi Baker

Heidi Baker has seen signs, wonders, and miracles. She has seen blind eyes opened, the deaf hear, and the dead raised. She has seen bread multiply and provision come just in the right time. She and her husband, Rolland, and her team have planted thousands of churches and ignited revival fires around the world. She has truly stewarded revival well. What she imparts to this generation is valuable to take to heart if we also want to be burning ones with signs and wonders following our lives. Intimacy with Jesus is the most important key to sustained revival. Prepare your heart to receive the key of intimacy from Heidi in the following pages.

If I could leave one piece of advice for this next generation, for my children, grandchildren, and their children, it would be that all fruitfulness flows from intimacy. We can't fulfill our destiny or do anything for God unless we are intimate with Him. Part of our destiny is fruitfulness and that comes by being close to

God. We need to let Daddy God love us, hold us in His arms, and pour out His love on us.

I was preaching at a conference on the Father Heart of God and at that time, I didn't really know the Father's heart. I was really nervous and I thought they had made a mistake by inviting me. I was there with people like John Arnott, Jack Frost, and Jack Winter. I wasn't even the right gender to be there and everything seemed so out of place. During worship, I was laid out on the carpet, crying out to God to help me. Then I saw Father God show up in a vision. He looked at me and smiled. When He did that, all the fear dissipated and I was ready to say yes to anything He wanted. I could yield myself totally to the Holy Spirit because I knew that He loved me no matter what. Then in the vision, He handed me some keys.

These keys opened different rooms. The first key opened a door that went into a massive warehouse full of food that I could use to feed the nations. He said to tell the church that if they align their hearts with God's that they too can have access to this key.

The next room was a really weird room because it had eyeballs, ears, lungs, hearts, feet, hands, and organs of the body lined up on a shelf. While I was looking at the eyes and the ears, I came to understand from His Spirit that it was the healing room. He said I would only have access to this room when He told me I could or else I would never sleep because of the heavy weight and great need for healing in the world. Since I have entered that room, many deaf have been healed. Every time we go into a village, I call the deaf to come forward. They come and God heals them. I don't have to fast about that or spend hours in intercession for this. I just know that I have access to the hearing because of what God has already shown me in the room. It's awesome to go into these rooms and others because now deaf ears open. Now we have keys to provision for food and God feeds thousands through our tiny little hands.

When He brought me to the last room, He told me that I would have to get down low to get into it. I remember the door was so low that I had to go on my hands and knees. When I put the key into the lock, my hand, then arm, and then whole body became the key. The key and my body became one. I crawled into that room and there was Jesus. When I looked at Him, I wept right there. I put my head on His chest and said that I never wanted to leave this room. I didn't care about the food, the healing, or anything else. I just wanted to stay there with Him day and night, just lying there on His chest. I just wanted to be there and never leave. I didn't care about anything but being in His presence.

But when I put my head on His heart, I heard Him say, "Go and get My lost bride. You can come in this room every day. You have full access here, you're welcome here any time." That's why I'm the way I am because I go into that room every day and then I go out looking for the lost bride. All true and lasting fruitfulness flows from intimacy with Jesus. Knowing Him is the point.

I feel like a lot of Christians even in this generation want everything quickly. They want someone to lay hands on them and instantly have an anointing. They want God to give them a stadium. They want the millions or the billions and God is saying, "I want you to yield, I want you to lay down, I want you to pay the price. I want you to give everything." I think a lot of people say "no" and miss out on their destiny. They don't want the hard things. But when we yield ourselves to God, He rips the "no" out of us.

I am calling this generation to go for it, to live lives of total surrender that flow from the place of intimacy with Jesus. I pray
that my ceiling would be your floor. I pray that you would have
greater depths of intimacy than I've ever known and that you
would reach more of the lost children than I could ever dream
of. I pray right now for the glory of God's love to hit your generation. I pray that you would be radically undone by who God
is and that you wouldn't be afraid to yield, to give yourself, to get
low, go slow, stop for the one, and get lower still.

I pray that you would see the shining eyes of the Father, that
you could see Him smiling on you, cheering you on. I pray that
you would give yourselves wholeheartedly to radical love with
Jesus and that you would be married to Him. I pray that you
would come into greater depths of intimacy than you have ever
known and that you would get so yielded that you become fully
possessed by Holy Spirit. I pray that you would be drenched by
the radical love that is poured out through the Father, Son, and
Holy Spirit.

11

AZUSA NOW

by Lou Engle

Lou Engle

As we cultivate intimacy with Jesus and stay connected to the true Source, we will see God do amazing things in and through our lives for His glory. We must always remember that as we seek to advance God's kingdom, we must remain in Him. With that said, what powerful, unstoppable, and dynamic explosions of God's love might occur when cultivating intimacy with Christ and stepping out in faith to see His kingdom come for our generation? One man who is stewarding and contending for great breakthrough for his and future generations is Lou Engle, co-founder of TheCall. This burning one shares how everything unfolded for him to gather a stadium of people together in Los Angeles in 2016 to re-dig the well of the Azusa Street Revival and go even deeper. He shares his story below.

In 1997, Promise Keepers put a million men on the mall in Washington D.C. to pray for America. It was a historic event in church history. When that happened, I began to declare that the hearts of the fathers are turning to the children, and that young people are turning back to their fathers. I had no idea what was being launched. This led to a supernatural series of events that emerged on September 2, 2000 where 400,000 young people gathered for twelve hours to cry out to God for awakening in America. This was catalytic and launched the movement of TheCall, which has been going for sixteen years now. I felt like God had given me a life assignment to raise up extended fasting and prayer all over the globe for the outpourings of the Holy Spirit.

I always knew that TheCall was some kind of John-the-Baptist-type movement because it was about fasting and prayer and raising up Nazarites. It was about turning America back to God. It was after this that I began to ask the question, "Has TheCall failed because we haven't seen America turn back to God?" The Lord spoke to me and said, "Lou, if it truly was a John-the-Baptist-type movement, you can bet there is a Jesus Movement coming." This made me believe there is another massive baptism of the Holy Spirit coming where stadiums will be filled with people coming to know Christ.

So I called my friend and shared this with him and he said, "Lou, do you remember the dream that I had where I received five sets of plane tickets and we could only fly United?" He knew it had to do with the fact that the church must unite because only a united church can heal a divided nation. He continued, "I was so concerned I'd miss the expiration date because in 1,080 days, the ticket would expire. I woke up and looked up 1,080 days from the day of my dream and guess what day it is? It's April 9, 2016, the 110th anniversary of the Azusa Street Revival."

From that moment on, I knew God had planned a date with His church. As we were praying about these things, my friend and I actually went to the Memorial Coliseum in Los Angeles. Somehow they let us get in there, and we claimed it for stadium Christianity. Then I got an e-mail from a young lady in Washington state who said, "I had this dream where I saw this huge stadium; it was both a football field and it was a baseball field. It was so vivid that I woke up and I checked to see if there were any stadiums that were both used for the Super Bowl and the World Series. There is only one, it's the Coliseum in Los Angeles. I think you're supposed to do TheCall Azusa there."

I was convinced in my heart that God wanted us to get the stadium, but I didn't have faith to raise the kind of money that it would cost to "buy the field." I was reading Matthew 13:44 where it says that when a man finds a treasure, he goes and hides it in a field and sells all that he has to buy that field with joy. There just comes a time when you want something more than anything else. For me, my calling has been revival for forty years. I would rather get revival than anything else except my own kids loving Jesus. I sensed the Lord say, "Sell the house to buy the field, the stadium for the treasure of the unity of the body of Christ and revival." I felt led to sell my house and use that money toward the stadium meeting. I share this not for it to be about some huge thing that I felt led to do—I literally just want revival.

I think we're at a point in America where everyone needs to begin to ask the question, "How much do we really want God in America?" It's time for the whole body of Christ to sell out for the greatest outpouring of the Holy Spirit. I believe we will begin to see the greatest awakening America has ever seen. We won't just talk about the past; we will talk about the future. A new Jesus Movement, a new Azusa Street. Let's work together to mobilize and release God's kingdom throughout the earth. Let's press in for God to do a massive breakthrough in our generation. It's not only what God did in Azusa then, it's what He wants to do in an even greater measure now. Oh God, give us another Jesus Movement I pray!

12

THE OPPORTUNITY OF A LIFETIME IS AT OUR DOOR

TAPPING INTO THE CURRENTS OF REVIVAL

See, I am doing a new thing!
Now it springs up; do you not perceive it?
I am making a way in the wilderness
and streams in the wasteland.

Isaiah 43:19

There is a window of opportunity set before us today. Let's not be like a generation of Israelites who missed out on their destiny because they hesitated to step into the things God had positioned them for (Numbers 13-14). These had a crucial window of time to step into their inheritance and to possess the Promised Land. They had a choice to see their circumstances from God's perspective and trust in His leading. Instead, they focused their attention on the giants in the land and allowed fear to cripple them. They even sought to stone Joshua and Caleb, the only two who actually believed in God's destiny for them.

It wasn't until after God rebuked the Israelites for their behavior toward His appointed leaders that they finally came to their senses and set out to respond to His earlier command in their lives to take the land. Only by this time, it was too late. Their opportunity as a generation to breakthrough into a new era had already passed them by. They missed out on their destiny because of a wrong perspective and not being ready to respond immediately to God's leading.

The giants in the Promised Land were real, and the giants we have to fight to take hold of our destiny are real. Rejection is real, poverty and sickness are real, and misunderstandings are real. But if God really is over all and if He is leading us, the surrounding circumstances are irrelevant, powerless in comparison with His greatness. Regardless of what giants we currently face, God is greater.

What if the Israelites had trusted in God and believed He wanted the best for them? If they had responded immediately to God's command to take possession of the Promised Land, would they have gained the victory? If they had all rallied behind Joshua and Caleb in support of overcoming the giants, would they have thrived in the Promised Land and had a different end to their story? What does this story say to us about the importance of not only saying yes to God when He leads, but also responding to Him in the moment as well?

A generation's destiny hung on a thread, on a moment. Just as the generation of Israelites who died in the desert missed out on their full destiny, so can we miss out on ours if we do not quickly respond to the leading of the Holy Spirit. What would have happened if people like Martin Luther King, Jr. did not respond to where God was leading him at the time? What if he would have hesitated, asked how, or lived in the fear of the giants surrounding him? If we hesitate to respond when God speaks to us, what will happen to those around us who need for us to live our destiny so that it brings a shift in their reality?

In June 1906, just months after the fire at Azusa Street was ignited, Frank Bartleman wrote the following:

> Opportunity once passed, is lost forever. There is a time when the tide is sweeping by our door. We may then plunge in and be carried to glorious blessing, success and victory. To stand shivering on the bank, timid, or paralyzed with stupor, at such a time, is to miss all, and most miserably fail, both for time and for eternity. Oh, our responsibility! The mighty tide of God's grace and favor is even now sweeping by us, in its prayer-directed course...It is time to 'get together,' and plunge in, individually and collectively. We are baptized 'in one Spirit, into one body,' - I Cor. 12:13. Let us lay aside all carnal contentions and divisions, that separate us from each other and from God. If we are of His body, we are 'one body.' The opportunity of a lifetime, of centuries, is at our door, to be eternally gained or lost. There is no time to hesitate. Act quickly, lest another take thy crown. Oh, church of Christ, awake! Be baptized with power. Then fly to rescue others. And to meet your Lord.[149]

Now is our time to arise and shine as a generation and to step into all that God has for us. This is our moment to make history.[150] Will we dive into all that God has for us in our generation, fixing our eyes on Jesus, the Author and Finisher of our faith?

I pray that you will be mantled with courage to jump into the impossibilities God sets before you where there are no other options but trusting in Him to catch you or learning how to fly. I declare that in the face of fear, you will have the determination to keep your eyes on Jesus. May you link arms together with the saints to partner with God for what He is about to pour out on all the earth. I pray that you will be like Joshua and Caleb, full of faith and ready to respond immediately to God as He leads you into the Promised Land of today. May you be so close to God that you know His ways, hear His voice, and only move when He moves.[151]

FORGING NEW PATHS

After the fearful and hesitant group of Israelites died off in the desert, it was time for a new generation to enter into the land that had been promised to them. Joshua and Caleb were the only two from the previous generation privileged to enter into the new era. When it was finally time for the Israelites to cross the Jordan and enter into the land of their destiny, specific directions were given to them.

> "When you see the ark of the covenant of the Lord your God, and the Levitical priests carrying it, you are to move out from your positions and follow it. Then you will know which way to go, since you have never been this way before." *Joshua 3:3-4*

If the Ark of the Covenant represents God's presence here, the Israelites were to follow its leading. No other road map would work, as they were going somewhere they had never been before.

We, too, are about to go off the map into great new adventures we have never been on before. The only way to pioneer to these new places with God will be to lean into Him and immediately follow the leading of the Holy Spirit. Let's not be content to go into the land of our destiny without His presence (Exodus 33). Let's always remember that knowing Jesus is our truest reward.

The stage has been set. The opportunity of a lifetime has been presented to our generation. The question is, will the hungry ones arise to take hold of Him and not let go until He comes in a most profound way, greater than ever before? Will you stop at nothing until you have taken hold of the One who has already paid the greatest price to take hold of you? Will you fulfill your destiny? He is increasing your hunger for Him and preparing to take you on the wildest ride of your life. Stay close to Him. He will hold you tight and surprise you beyond what you could ever dream.

13

STEPPING INTO
THE IMPOSSIBLE

by Bill Johnson

Bill Johnson

Many saints have gone before us and paid a great price to pioneer into new spiritual territories. They have paved the way for us to access and tap into a greater measure of our God-given inheritance through the risks they have taken. What an awesome opportunity we have been given to build on their momentum and go even further in our day. One man who knows about momentum is Bill Johnson, senior leader at Bethel Church. He is a fifth-generation pastor who understands the importance of tapping into the power of the testimony and honoring those who have come before. May the wisdom he releases below inspire you to throw off any weight that hinders and run with great passion and endurance, fixing your eyes on Jesus, the Author and the Finisher of your faith (see Hebrews 12).

Years ago somebody asked Oral Roberts why he saw so many miracles but the person asking the question didn't. Roberts said something like, "That's easy. If God doesn't answer my prayers, I am done with. I don't have a plan B. I don't have another option." In other words, live in such a way that unless God shows up, what you are attempting to do is bound to fail. This kind of abandonment is the nature of the gospel.

Here's how we are "co-missioned" into this assignment. He said, "Go into a city. Find a place to stay. Don't bring any money. Don't take enough clothing that you can take care of yourself for extended periods of time. Make yourself vulnerable in your abandonment to My purposes so that unless I show up, provide, and direct, it will not work."

One of the things that keeps us in a place of ongoing vulnerability and trust before the Lord is to stay aware of an assignment we cannot accomplish. Do you ever pray better when you are overwhelmed? Some of my greatest prayers are short like, "Help!"

And they are powerful prayers too, because I am moved in these prayers. I am overwhelmed. It is one thing to be overwhelmed with difficulties. It is another thing to be overwhelmed by an assignment I cannot do. Living conscious of what is required of my life keeps me in a place of abandonment and trust, which is where I am the safest.

The safest place for believers is on the frontlines of their assigned battle. The most dangerous place to be is in a place of trying to protect what we have been given. It may seem more logical to think we are supposed to guard and to shepherd what God has entrusted us with. But we cannot stop there as though occupation were the goal. The purpose of occupation is advancement until Jesus says it is over, and He comes back. Until that moment comes, there is an assignment to see the kingdoms of this world become the kingdoms of our Lord and of His Christ (Revelation 11:15-16). We have an assignment to see the glory of God fill the earth as the waters cover the sea (Habakkuk 2:14).

The Lord said to Joshua, "Be strong and of good courage. You are going to give these people the land." He gave Moses and other ones a great commission. When the Lord gave them an impossible assignment, He would follow it by saying, "And certainly I will be with you." God majors in giving us assignments we can't do on our own. He says we are required to do something impossible and then says that He will be with us. In other words, the presence of the Lord qualifies us for the impossible. And because of the presence of the Lord in our lives, we are *required* to do the impossible. It is not an option.

The original assignment that Joshua received was to lead Israel into the land of promises and to take the inheritance that belonged to each tribe of Israel. Joshua did what he was supposed to do in this lifetime, but the generation of Israelites following him had not entered into the fullness of the Promised Land yet. When Joshua died, some territory that God had declared to be theirs was still not in their possession. Not until David came along several hundred years later did Israel get the remainder of the land. Joshua and the elders passed the baton to the next generation. That generation's assignment was to carry on what their fathers had done, which was to get the entire land for Israel. But instead of doing that, they settled and occupied the incomplete land they had taken.

The model of Joshua and the elders who outlived him passing the baton to the next generation is exactly what has followed every revival for 2000 years. Courageous leaders brought significant breakthrough and then passed the baton to the next group, who dialed it down to what was humanly possible and built monuments to the heroes in the previous generation.

The Azusa Street Revival brought such an awareness of the One who invades supernaturally. There was a shift of understanding of what was possible. Everything that they had seen in previous revivals was wonderful, but it was only the building blocks. The miraculous became much more pronounced at Azusa. The presence of God was the dominating feature. The Holy Spirit would come, and there would be such sensitivity to His presence. Revival fire went from Azusa Street all over the country and then around the world. Many other places in the world broke out in revival at the same time as Azusa. It was like a sovereign breath of God all over the earth. It was really quite extraordinary. In the last century, there has been a dramatic increase in miracles, signs and wonders. Miracles are wonderful displays of the Father's heart for people. God is leading us into even greater breakthroughs today.

This means we have a momentum in the Spirit. We have to be people who absolutely trust God. We have to put ourselves in a place of vulnerability so that we have nowhere to turn, but to God. Jesus has so yoked us with an impossible assignment that we either stay yielded and under the influence of that assignment, or we reduce ministry to what is humanly possible.

Jesus gave His disciples an assignment that was absolutely impossible. He also gave His disciples absolute authority for anything that was needed in this impossible assignment.

> Then he called his twelve disciples together, and gave them power and authority over all demons, and to cure diseases. (Luke 9:1 *NKJV*)

He also painted a picture that allowed them to see their place in history.

> Then he turned to his disciples and said privately, "Blessed are the eyes that see what you see. For I tell you that many prophets and kings wanted to see what you see but did not see it, and to hear what you hear but did not hear it." (Luke 10:23-24 *NKJV*)

If we as parents and grandparents can raise a generation that understands what has happened throughout history, it will be powerful. He essentially said, "Listen, this generation that you are alive in is so significant that the Solomons, Davids, Elijahs, and Ezekiels that preceded you saw in the Spirit something that was coming, but I gave them no access to it. I am now giving that access to you. Keep it in perspective."

All of history has been building to this divine moment that you live in. Something happens to a generation that wakes up to realize this is the moment the prophets have been speaking into. This is the hour that they have been serving for. Others before me were far greater than me in their faith and relationship with God, yet they were not allowed to see what I have been allowed to see with my own eyes. What does that require of me?

I cannot give up on my assignment of invading the impossible and of absolute abandonment to God and His purposes. I only get one shot at this life. I only get one chance to make my contribution to the transformation of planet earth for the glory of King Jesus. That is the assignment.

The momentum in the Spirit is accelerating. How does it accelerate? By keeping in context all the generations who sowed into something that I can now taste of because I am to execute the administration of God's purposes on a planet. It is not about me. It is not about this generation. It is about the call and the purposes of God for a planet. He has been building it for hundreds of years—setting the stage for the generation that would step into His full destiny and call. That is all of us. This is it. This is the commission. Will we step into the impossible today?

We've been given an anointing that invades the impossibilities in others' lives to bring freedom. We carry the presence of another world. We carry a divine assignment. Even with his wealth,

Solomon was not allowed to taste of what we have today. David with his insights and heavenly experiences was not allowed to taste what we can see. Elijah and John the Baptist longed for it. But none of them could experience what you and I see on a daily basis. We have had all kinds of cancer healed. We have seen deaf ears opened, deliverance from devils, torment taken off of people's lives, and still others set free after generations of bondage. These are things past generations were not allowed to see.

Today there is a grace on our lives, something that we have paid a price for and are now in a position to give away, an inheritance acquired through personal breakthrough that will bring about a change for every generation from this point on. Is it possible that a Holy Spirit boldness, like the disciples prayed for in Acts, would come upon us, to position us to take new territory in the Promised Land and give it as an inheritance to someone else for free? I believe the answer is a resounding *yes!*

14

A NEW JESUS REVOLUTION

We truly are on the verge of a new Jesus Revolution. The next great awakening is coming upon us. In this new season, it will be important to fix our eyes on Jesus, regardless of what is going on around us—no matter how strange or exhilarating. In the midst of the revival, the leadership at Azusa encouraged their friends to keep their "eyes on Jesus and not on the manifestations."[152] Jesus also emphasized the importance of relationship with Him as the true source of miracles when He said in Matthew 7:21-23,

> "Not everyone who says to me, 'Lord, Lord,' will enter the kingdom of heaven, but only the one who does the will of my Father who is in heaven. Many will say to me on that day, 'Lord, Lord, did we not prophesy in your name and in your name drive out demons and in your name perform many miracles?' Then I will tell them plainly, 'I never knew you. Away from me, you evildoers!'"

It normally wouldn't seem like prophesying, casting out demons, and performing miracles are actions of "evildoers" or of those who practice lawlessness. However, Jesus said it right here. If we do any of these signs and wonders outside of *knowing* Him, it's dangerous. God is calling us both to be intimate with Jesus *and* to advance His kingdom with signs and wonders. These things must always come together.

As Heidi shared earlier, intimacy with Jesus is one of the most important keys to sustaining revival and to finishing well. There are no shortcuts to intimacy with Jesus. Building our connection with Him takes time. As we prepare to go after stadiums of people getting saved, serving the poor, raising the dead, and greater signs and wonders, let's remember how important it is to stay connected to the Source.

At the beginning of the day and at the end of it all, knowing Jesus is still what matters most.[153] Great exploits for the kingdom of God await us. As we draw closer to God, He will mantle us with courage to step out in great faith to do the impossible. In whatever may come, let's always remember that it's all about Jesus. Let's be a community of burning ones who are so possessed by His love that we, like the early saints at Azusa, ignite a fire that burns for generations to come.

I pray that as you participate in the greatest awakening of your lifetime, you are drawn to spend even more time in His presence. I pray that you would be marked with a burning passion for Jesus like never before and that fresh fire would be ignited inside of you. Throughout all the storms and thrills of life, I pray that Jesus would always be on your mind and that there would never be "a thousand other things" before Him. May He be your first and all-consuming passion. I pray that you will be melted in perfect union with the most intimate lover you will ever know. May He be your portion, your prize, and your obsession forever. May a new Jesus Revolution emerge where the name of Jesus is celebrated and where His name is made famous once again.

NOTES

1. If you want to dig deeper, see Frank Bartleman's *How Pentecost Came to Los Angeles*, Cecil M. Robeck, Jr.'s *The Azusa Street Mission & Revival*, Allan Anderson's *Spreading Fires*, the series Larry Martin put together on the history of Azusa, books by Vinson Synan and others. I draw heavily on Frank Bartleman's work and on the original newspaper of the Azusa Street Revival called *The Apostolic Faith* because these are some of the best primary sources written closest to or during the revival. In order to preserve the original documents, all of the quotes are taken from primary sources with any mistakes the author made left unchanged.

PREFACE: THE CURRENT OF REVIVAL IS SWEEPING BY OUR DOOR

2. Smith Wigglesworth, *Ever Increasing Faith* (Springfield, MO: Gospel Publishing House, 1924), 129-130. "For many years the Lord has been moving me on and keeping me from spiritual stagnation. When I was in the Wesleyan Methodist Church I was sure I was saved and sure I was all right. The Lord said to me, 'Come out,' and I came out. When I was with the people known as the Brethren I was sure I was all right now. But the Lord said, 'Come out.' Then I went into the Salvation Army. At that time it was full of life and there were revivals everywhere. But the Salvation Army went into natural things and the great revivals that they had in those early days ceased. The Lord said to me, 'Come out,' and I came out. I have had to come out three times since. I believe that this Pentecostal revival that we are now in is the best thing that the Lord has on the earth today, and yet I believe that God has something out of this that is going to be still better. God has no use for any man who is not hungering and thirsting for yet more of Himself and His righteousness."

3. David J. du Plessis and Bob Slosser, *A Man Called Mr. Pentecost* (Plainfield, NJ: Logos International, 1977), 2-3. David du Plessis

later went on to be a significant influence for the charismatic movement and traveled the world releasing the Pentecostal blessing to many. There are variations of this personal prophecy and some debates about the exact wording. See Roberts Liardon, *The Smith Wigglesworth Prophecy & the Greatest Revival of All Time* (New Kensington, PA: Whitaker House, 2013) for more on this discussion.

4. Bob Jones, Interview June 2007 with Abiding Glory Ministries, Washington DC, accessible https://youtu.be/EtWKDOa2Y7w (accessed January 25, 2016). See also Bob Jones, Divine Encounters interview on Patricia King's XP media at https://youtu.be/4g6ZZ-ChTTc (accessed January 25, 2016).

5. Frank Bartleman, *How Pentecost Came to Los Angeles: As it Was in the Beginning.* 2nd edition (Los Angeles, CA: Frank Bartleman, originally April 1925), 39 and now printed by Christian Classic Ethereal Library (Grand Rapids, MI) accessible http://www.ccel.org/ccel/bartleman/los.pdf (accessed January 25, 2016).

1. CATCHING THE WAVE OF THE SPIRIT

6. In *Strong's Concordance*, see Hebrew word #5749 at http://lexiconcordance.com/hebrew/5749.html (accessed February 2, 2016).

7. Home of Peace Guest Book 1906-1910 original handwritten copy researched at and courtesy of the Home of Peace.

2. PIONEERS WHO PAVED THE WAY

8. To learn more about well digging see Lou Engle's *Digging the Wells of Revival: Reclaiming Your Historic Inheritance Through Prophetic Intercession* with Catherine Paine (Shippensburg, PA: Revival Press, 1998).

9. Cecil M. Robeck, Jr., *The Azusa Street Mission and Revival: The Birth of the Global Pentecostal Movement* (Nashville, TN: Nelson Reference and Electronic, 2006), 42-43.

10. Vinson Synan and Charles R. Fox, Jr., *William J. Seymour: Pioneer of the Azusa Street Revival* (Alachua, FL: Bridge Logos Foundation, 2012), 57-58.

11. "The Old-Time Pentecost," *The Apostolic Faith*, 1:1 (312 Azusa Street, Los Angeles, CA: September, 1906), 1. The reason this author may have been Seymour is because they decided not to include names on the articles because they wanted only God to receive the glory.

12. The early 1900s were a sacred time set apart by God for all who were hungry to partake and invite a mighty outpouring of the Spirit. For more on sacred time, see Jennifer A. Miskov, "Coloring Outside the Lines: Pentecostal Parallels with Expressionism. The Work of the Spirit in Place, Time, and Secular Society?" *Journal of Pentecostal Theology 19* (2010) 94–117.

13. Allan Anderson, *Spreading Fires: The Missionary Nature of Early Pentecostalism* (London: SCM Press, 2007), 77-89.

14. Abrams, Minnie F., *The Baptism of the Holy Ghost and Fire*, (Kedgaon, India: Pandita Ramabai Mukti Mission, 1906), 1.

15. Abrams, *The Baptism of the Holy Ghost and Fire*, 2-3.

16. Anderson, *Spreading Fires*, 77-89.

17. Report by Mrs. M. Baxter in *The Eleventh Hour* in S.B. Shaw, *The Great Revival in Wales* (Chicago, IL: S.B. Shaw Publisher, 1905), 13-14.

18. Bartleman, *How Pentecost Came to Los Angeles*, 16. "June 17, [1905] I went to Los Angeles to attend a meeting at the First Baptist Church. They were waiting on God for an outpouring of the Spirit there. Their pastor, Joseph Smale, had just returned from Wales. He had been in touch with the revival and Evan Roberts, and was on fire to have the same visitation and blessing come to his own church in Los Angeles. I found this meeting of an exact piece with my own vision, burden, and desire, and spent two hours in the church in prayer, before the evening service. Meetings were being held every day and night there and God was present."

19. Jennifer A. Miskov, "The Liturgy of the Welsh Revival and the Azusa Street Revival: Connections, Similarities and Development" in *Scripting Pentecost* by eds. A.J. Swaboda and Mark Cartledge (New York, NY: Ashgate, 2016).

20. Bartleman, *How Pentecost Came to Los Angeles*, 19, 22. "Pastor Smale has returned from Wales, where he was in touch with Evan Roberts, and the revival. He registers his conviction that Los Angeles will soon be shaken by the mighty power of God. A wonderful work of the Spirit has broken out here in Los Angeles, California, preceded by a deep preparatory work of prayer and expectation. Conviction is rapidly spreading among the people, and they are rallying from all over the city to the meetings at Pastor Smale's church. Already these meetings are beginning to 'run themselves.' Souls are being saved all over the house, while the meeting sweeps on unguided by human hands. The tide is rising rapidly, and we are anticipating wonderful things. Soul travail is becoming an important feature of the work, and we are being swept away beyond sectarian barriers. The fear of God is coming upon the people, a very spirit of burning. Sunday night the meeting ran on until the small hours of the next morning. Pastor Smale is prophesying of wonderful things to come. He prophesies the speedy return of the apostolic 'gifts' to the church. Los Angeles is a veritable Jerusalem. Just the place for a mighty work of God to begin. I have been expecting just such a display of divine power for some time. Have felt it might break out any hour. Also that it was liable to come where least expected, that God might get the glory. Pray for a 'Pentecost.'"

21. Ibid., 38. Bartleman also said, "I started a little cottage prayer meeting where we could have more liberty to pray and wait on the Lord…He came and filled our little cottage with a cloud of glory until I could scarcely bear His presence."

22. See also the following verses for more examples about impartation: Deuteronomy 34:9, 1 Samuel 10, Exodus 17:5-6, 2 Kings 2:14, 4:29, 13:21, Matthew 8:8-11, Romans 1:11-12, Acts 6:6, 8:19-20, 19:11-13, 1 Timothy 4:14, 5:21-22, 2 Timothy 1:6, 2:2.

23. Around this same time, G. Campbell Morgan's little tract on the "Revival in Wales" spread the fire in the churches in Los Angeles, as did S. B. Shaw's book, *The Great Revival* in Wales (Chicago, IL: S.B. Shaw Publisher, 1905).

24. Bartleman, *How Pentecost Came to Los Angeles*, 15. In May, 1905, he wrote the following article: "My soul is on fire as I read of the glorious work of grace in Wales. The 'seven thousand' in the land, who have kept company with the 'spared ones' (Ezek. 9), and who

114

have been crying and sighing because of the abomination and desolation in the land, the decay of vital piety in the body of Christ, may well be excused for rejoicing at such a time and prospect as this, when God is once more moving in the earth. But where are the men who will 'stir themselves up to take hold on God?' Let our watchword at this time be 'California for Christ.'"

25. Ibid., 39. "Flesh and blood cannot inherit the kingdom of God." - Christian Harvester.

26. Ibid.,19-20.

27. Ibid., 19-20. "We prayed for a spirit of revival for Pasadena until the burden became well nigh unbearable. I cried out like a woman in birth-pangs. The Spirit was interceding through us. Finally the burden left us. After a little time of quiet waiting a great calm settled down upon us. Then suddenly, without premonition the Lord Jesus himself revealed himself to us. He seemed to stand directly between us, so close we could have reached out our hand and touched him."

28. Ibid., 38.

29. Ibid., 17-18. "I had written a letter to Evan Roberts in Wales, asking them to pray for us in California. I now received a reply that they were doing so, which linked us up with the revival there. The letter read as follows: 'My dear brother in the faith: Many thanks for your kind letter. I am impressed of your sincerity and honesty of purpose...' We were much encouraged to know that they were praying for us in Wales."

30. Ibid., 36.

31. Bartleman, *How Pentecost Came to Los Angeles*, 22. Azusa Street historian Cecil M. Robeck, Jr. states "the subject of revival was in the air when William Seymour arrived. Since 1904 many Christians in Los Angeles had been hearing about a great revival in Wales" in Robeck, Jr., *Azusa Street Mission and Revival*, 57.

32. Ibid., 35. "For several days I had an impression another letter was coming from Evan Roberts. It soon came, and read as follows: 'Loughor, Wales, Nov. 14, '05. My dear comrade... I pray God to hear your prayer, to keep your faith strong, and to save California. I remain, your brother in the fight. Evan Roberts.' This was the third letter I had received from Wales, from Evan Roberts, and I feel their prayers had much to do with our final victory in California."

33. Ibid., 31-32.

3. THE AZUSA STREET STORY

34. Charles W. Shumway, "A Study of 'The Gift of Tongues'" (master's thesis, University of Southern California at Los Angeles, 1914), 173 in Vinson Synan and Charles R. Fox, Jr., *William J. Seymour: Pioneer of the Azusa Street Revival* (Alachua, FL: Bridge Logos Foundation, 2012), 31. See also Larry Martin, *The Life and Ministry of William J. Seymour* (Joplin, MO: Christian Life Books, 1999), 70.
35. Robeck, Jr., *The Azusa Street Mission and Revival*, 33. See also Cecil M. Robeck, Jr. "William Joseph Seymour," *The New International Dictionary of Pentecostal and Charismatic Movements*, Revised and Expanded Edition, eds. Stanley M. Burgess and E.M. Van Der Maas (Grand Rapids, MI: Zondervan, 2002), 1053-1058. It is likely that Seymour studied at Knapp's "God's Bible School." He saw alignment with Knapp in three areas: racial integration, premillennialism, and his taking divine revelations seriously where others in Seymour's circles discarded these. See Synan and Fox, Jr., *William J. Seymour: Pioneer of the Azusa Street Revival*, 37-40.
36. Robeck, Jr., "William Joseph Seymour," *The New International Dictionary of Pentecostal and Charismatic Movements*, 1053-1058. The church was called Evening Light Saints (later the Church of God Reformation Movement).
37. Roberts Liardon, "William J. Seymour," at http://www.godsgenerals. com/person_w_seymour.htm (accessed January 25, 2016). See also Bartleman, *How Pentecost Came to Los Angeles*, 44.
38. Synan and Fox, Jr., *William J. Seymour: Pioneer of the Azusa Street Revival*, 46-47. This was either Charles Price Jones or Charles Harrison Mason, both of whom were prominent black ministers. Both of these men were asked to leave the Baptist church because of their stance on sanctification as a second work of grace. They ended up forming the Church of God in Christ.
39. John G. Lake, "Origin of the Apostolic Faith Movement," *The Pentecostal Outlook* (September 1932), 3. This article was originally written in 1911, found in Larry Martin, *The Life and Ministry of*

116

William J. Seymour (Joplin, MO: Christian Life Books, 1999), 141-142.

40. Cecil M. Robeck, Jr., "Bonnie Brae Street Cottage," *The New International Dictionary of Pentecostal and Charismatic Movements*, Revised and Expanded Edition, eds. Stanley M. Burgess and E.M. Van Der Maas (Grand Rapids, MI: Zondervan, 2002), 437-438.

41. Vinson Synan, "The Azusa Street Revival: Celebrating 100 Years," *Assemblies of God Heritage* 25:4 (Winter 2005-2006), 7.

42. Robeck, Jr., *The Azusa Street Mission and Revival*, 66.

43. Larry Martin, *The Life and Ministry of William J. Seymour* (Joplin, MO: Christian Life Books, 1999), 142 in reference to Charles W. Shumway, "*A Critical History of Glossolalia*," unpublished Ph.D. dissertation (Boston University, 1919), 115.

44. Martin, *The Life and Ministry of William J. Seymour*, 142 in reference to Shumway, "*A Critical History of Glossolalia*," 115.

45. At this point in time, people can visit the Bonnie Brae House by appointment for free. There are also options to stay the night with a group for a fee. You can access the phone number by doing a search for the house online.

46. Robeck, Jr., *The Azusa Street Mission and Revival*, 67.

47. Ibid.

48. Robeck, Jr., "William Joseph Seymour," 1053-1058.

49. "When the day of Pentecost came, they were all together in one place. Suddenly a sound like the blowing of a violent wind came from heaven and filled the whole house where they were sitting. They saw what seemed to be tongues of fire that separated and came to rest on each of them. All of them were filled with the Holy Spirit and began to speak in other tongues as the Spirit enabled them." Acts 2:1-4

50. Martin, *The Life and Ministry of William J. Seymour*, 146 in reference to Charles W. Shumway, "A Study of 'The Gift of Tongues'" (master's thesis, University of Southern California at Los Angeles, 1914), 175.

51. Jennie Moore, "Music from Heaven," *The Apostolic Faith* 1:8 (312 Azusa Street, Los Angeles, CA: May, 1907), 3. Here is the full version below: "It has been often related how the Pentecost fell in Los Angeles over a year ago in a cottage prayer meeting. Sister Jennie Moore who was in that meeting and received her Pentecost

gives her testimony as follows: 'For years before this wonderful experience came to us, we as a family, were seeking to know the fulnes of God, and He was filling us with His presence until we could hardly contain the power. I had never seen a vision in my life, but one day as we prayed there passed before me three white cards, each with two names thereon, and but for fear I could have given them, as I saw every letter distinctly. On April 9, 1906, I was praising the Lord from the depths of my heart at home, and when the evening came and we attended the meeting the power of God fell and I was baptized in the Holy Ghost and fire, with the evidence of speaking in tongues. During the day I had told the Father that although I wanted to sing under the power that I was willing to do whatever He willed, and at the meeting when the power came on me I was reminded of the three cards which had passed me in vision months ago. As I thought thereon and looked to God, it seemed as if a vessel broke within me and water surged up through my being, which when it reached my mouth came out in a torrent of speech in the languages which God had given me. I remembered the names on the cards: French, Spanish, Latin, Greek, Hebrew, Hindustani, and as the message came with power, so quick that but a few words would have been recognized, interpretation of each message followed in English, the name of the language would come to me. I sang under the power of the Spirit in many languages, the interpretation both words and music which I had never before heard, and in the home where the meeting was being held, the Spirit led me to the piano, where I played and sang under inspiration, although I had not learned to play. In these ways God is continuing to use me to His glory ever since that wonderful day, and I praise Him for the privilege of being a witness for Him under the Holy Ghost's power.'"

52. Martin, *The Life and Ministry of William J. Seymour*, 148.
53. Stanley M. Horton, "The Azusa Street Revival According to Stanley Horton," *Assemblies of God Heritage Magazine* 25:4 (Winter 2005-2006), 30.
54. Bartleman, *How Pentecost Came to Los Angeles*, 47. "They had been tarrying very earnestly for some time for an outpouring. A handful of colored and white saints had been waiting there daily…There was a general spirit of humility manifested in the meeting. They were

taken up with God." Bartleman also said how on "Sunday, April 15, the Lord called me to ten days of special prayer. I felt greatly burdened but had no idea of what He had particularly in mind. But He had a work for me, and wanted to prepare me for it."

55. Robeck, Jr., *The Azusa Street Mission and Revival*, 6. On April 18, 1906, news of the emerging revival made it into the *Los Angeles Daily Times*, the same day of the great San Francisco earthquake.

56. Bartleman, *How Pentecost Came to Los Angeles*, 47-48. "Here they had rented an old frame building, formerly a Methodist church, in the center of the city, now a long time out of use for meetings. It had become a receptacle for old lumber, plaster, etc. They had cleared space enough in the surrounding dirt and debris to lay some planks on top of empty nail kegs, with seats enough for possibly thirty people, if I remember rightly. These were arranged in a square, facing one another. Discernment was not perfect, and the enemy got some advantage, which brought reproach to the work, but the saints soon learned to 'take the precious from the vile.' The combined forces of hell were set determinedly against us in the beginning. It was not all blessing. In fact the fight was terrific. The devil scraped the country for crooked spirits, as always, to destroy the work if possible. But the fire could not be smothered. Strong saints were gathered together to the help of the Lord. Gradually the tide arose in victory. But from a small beginning, a very little flame."

57. Robeck, Jr., *The Azusa Street Mission and Revival*, 81-82.

58. Ibid., 154. From a different perspective, James Dunn notices Spirit baptism as the 'most distinctive aspect of Pentecostal theology' in his *Baptism in the Holy Spirit: A Re-examination of the New Testament Teaching on the Gift of the Spirit in relation to Pentecostalism today*, (SCM Press Ltd, London: 1970), introduction page.

59. Bartleman, *How Pentecost Came to Los Angeles*, 58-59.

60. Synan, "The Azusa Street Revival: Celebrating 100 Years," 8-9. Or twenty-four hundred square feet.

61. Synan and Fox, Jr., *William J. Seymour: Pioneer of the Azusa Street Revival*, 57-58.

62. Unknown author, "Pentecostal Faith Line," *The Apostolic Faith* 1:1 (312 Azusa Street, Los Angeles, CA: September, 1906), 3. "There are a dozen or more Christian workers who are devoting their time to the salvation of souls, having been called of God in

other lines of employment to devote their time in praying with the sick, preaching, working with souls at the altar, etc. We believe in the faith line for Christian workers, and no collections are taken. During the four months, meetings have been running constantly, and yet without working day and night and without purse or scrip, the workers have all been kept well and provided with food and raiment. Workers who have received calls to foreign lands are going out, the Lord providing the means with no needs being presented. The ones that give, give as the Lord speaks to them and do not want their names mentioned.".…A sister who was called to Oakland had her faith tested as to her fare, as the time was near and she had not received it. That night she was caught away in the Spirit and when the Lord brought her back, the words came to her, 'If I can carry you around Los Angeles without a body, I can take you to Oakland without a fare.' So that day she received the money."

4. ENCOUNTER

63. Unknown author, "The Old-Time Pentecost," *The Apostolic Faith*, 1:1 (312 Azusa Street, Los Angeles, CA: September, 1906), 1. Speaking in tongues played a major part in the Azusa Street Revival even from the very beginning. Robert Mapes Anderson also comments on this in his Vision of the Disinherited: The Making of American Pentecostalism (New York and Oxford: Oxford University Press, 1979), 4. The development of the initial evidence doctrine changed and was modified over the years within various Pentecostal groups.

64. See Jennifer A. Miskov, *Life on Wings: The Forgotten Life and Theology of Carrie Judd Montgomery* (Cleveland, TN: CPT Press, 2012), 110-114. See also Miskov, "Coloring Outside the Lines," 94–117. Some of this section on Azusa Street is influenced from this article. For a good overview of the revival, see Robeck, Jr., *The Azusa Street Mission and Revival*.

65. Maggie Geddis, "Found the Pearl of Great Price," *The Apostolic Faith* 1:6 (312 Azusa Street, Los Angeles, CA: February-March, 1907), 4.

66. Bartleman, *How Pentecost Came to Los Angeles*, 59-60.

67. This section is influenced by Jennifer A. Miskov, *Spirit Flood: Rebirth of Spirit Baptism for the 21st Century (In Light of the Azusa Street Revival and the Life of Carrie Judd Montgomery)* (Birmingham, UK: Silver to Gold), 2010.

68. Carrie Judd Montgomery, "'The Promise of the Father.' A Personal Testimony," *Triumphs of Faith* 28:7 (Oakland, CA: July 1908), 146.

69. Carrie Judd Montgomery, "A Year with the Comforter," *Triumphs of Faith* 29:7 (Oakland, CA: July 1909), 145-149. It must be noted that she received prayer for Spirit baptism before this and she experienced an increase in God's presence but without the gift of tongues. She placed the date of her true Spirit baptism alongside the time she also spoke in tongues.

70. Carrie Judd Montgomery, "Miraculously Healed by the Lord Thirty Years Ago," Latter Rain Evangel 2:1 (October 1909), 9-10 and in *Triumphs of Faith* 28:7 (Oakland, CA: July 1908), 145.

71. Carrie Judd Montgomery, *Under His Wings: The Story of My Life*, (Los Angeles: Stationers Corporation, 1936), 164.

72. Montgomery, "'The Promise of the Father,'" 146.

73. Montgomery, "A Year with the Comforter," 145-149 and Montgomery, *Under His Wings*, 170.

74. Carrie Judd Montgomery, "The Life on Wings: The Possibilities of Pentecost," *The Latter Rain Evangel* 3:3 (December 1910), 22 and also Carrie Judd Montgomery, "Life on Wings. The Possibilities of Pentecost," *Triumphs of Faith* 32:8 (Oakland, CA: August 1912), 169-177.

75. Carrie Judd Montgomery, "Together in Love," *Triumphs of Faith* 28:9 (Oakland, CA: September 1908), 193-195 and "'By this all Men Shall know,'" *Triumphs of Faith* 28:11 (Oakland, CA: November 1908), 241-243.

76. Montgomery, "Life on Wings. The Possibilities of Pentecost," 169-177. This article was taken from an address she delivered at the Stone Church in Chicago in 1910 and revised by the author (CJM).

5. THE FIRE SPREADS

77. Unknown author, "Raised from the Dead," *The Apostolic Faith* 1:9 (312 Azusa Street, Los Angeles, CA: June to September, 1907), 4.
78. Synan, "The Azusa Street Revival: Celebrating 100 Years," 10.
79. Ibid., 8.
80. *The Apostolic Faith* 1:8 (312 Azusa Street, Los Angeles, CA: May, 1907), 3.
81. See Allan Anderson, *Spreading Fires: The Missionary Nature of Early Pentecostalism* (London: SCM Press, 2007) to learn more about the missionary nature of early Pentecostalism as well as the early revival fires that emerged around the world at a similar time or even before the flame at Azusa was ignited.
82. Robeck, Jr., *The Azusa Street Mission and Revival*, 7-8.
83. Robeck, Jr., "Azusa Street Revival," 348.
84. Roberts Liardon, *The Azusa Street Revival: When the Fire Fell* (Shippensburg, PA: Destiny Image, 2006), 154-155.
85. *The Apostolic Faith* 1:6 (312 Azusa Street, Los Angeles, CA: February-March, 1907), 8.
86. *The Apostolic Faith* 1:1 (312 Azusa Street, Los Angeles, CA: Los Angeles, September 1906), 1.
87. Unknown author, "Fire Falling at Hermon," *The Apostolic Faith* 1:1 (312 Azusa Street, Los Angeles, CA: Los Angeles, September 1906), 1.
88. *The Apostolic Faith* 1:3 (312 Azusa Street, Los Angeles, CA: November, 1906), 1. "The blind man who was saved and had his sight restored was saved because of hearing a few praying in tongues in a cottage meeting. He was a sinner; a very profane man, and was convicted because of tongues. Praise God for His marvelous works to the children of men."
89. E.W. Sterling, *The Apostolic Faith* 1:6 (312 Azusa Street, Los Angeles, CA: February-March, 1907), 8. "On January 31, while attending a little cottage prayer meeting, the fire fell on me and there I was for about two hours and a half praying and singing in tongues. The Lord showed be [sic] a vision of heaven. The buildings looked as if they were inlaid with diamonds. I saw the people coming, and they came to one with authority sitting with a great book. He turned the leaves and passed the people who had

not on the robe of righteousness. The Lord showed me that we as Christians should preach to them."

90. Unknown author, "A Happy Family, " *The Apostolic Faith* 1:9 (312 Azusa Street, Los Angeles, CA: September, 1907), 2.

91. Unknown author, "Pentecost in Australia," *The Apostolic Faith* 2:13 (312 Azusa Street, Los Angeles, CA: May, 1908), 1.

92. Unknown author, "At Azusa Mission," *The Apostolic Faith* 1:8 (312 Azusa Street, Los Angeles, CA: May, 1907), 2.

93. Unknown author, "Pentecost in Australia," *The Apostolic Faith* 2:13 (312 Azusa Street, Los Angeles, CA: May, 1908), 1. In February of 1907, at a cottage meeting in Melbourne, a man was baptized by the Holy Spirit and spoke in tongues while "some fell under the power of God, and a great awe came over the meeting."

6. THE FIRE BURNS DEEP

94. Bartleman, *How Pentecost Came to Los Angeles*, 97-98.

95. *The Apostolic Faith* 1:11 (312 Azusa Street, Los Angeles, CA: October to January, 1908), 4.

96. Unknown author, "Everywhere Preaching the Word," *The Apostolic Faith* 1:10 (312 Azusa Street, Los Angeles, CA: September, 1907), 1. "From Hermon, one sister saw fire issuing out of the tabernacle, as it were a tongue of fire. Her daughter also saw it."

97. Bartleman, *How Pentecost Came to Los Angeles*, 64.

98. Unknown author, "Beginning of World Wide Revival," *The Apostolic Faith* 1:5 (312 Azusa Street, Los Angeles, CA: January, 1907), 1. "In the meetings, you see the holy joy of the Lord in the countenances, and people are melted in the presence of the Lord, filled with His praises."

99. *The Apostolic Faith* 1:4 (312 Azusa Street, Los Angeles, CA: December, 1906), 1.

100. Ibid.

101. *The Apostolic Faith* 2:13 (312 Azusa Street, Los Angeles, CA: May, 1908), 2. "He wants us to have not only the thunder but the lightning. The Holy Ghost is lightning. He strikes men down with conviction, slays and makes alive."

7. FLOWING WITH THE HOLY SPIRIT

102. Bartleman, *How Pentecost Came to Los Angeles*, 58.
103. Ibid., "The ministers were servants, according to the true meaning of the word. We did not honor men for their advantage, in means or education, but rather for their God-given 'gifts.'"
104. Robeck, Jr. notes that "The upstairs space at the mission was often shared with other boarders who contributed to the work of the mission in return for a room," in Robeck, Jr., "William Joseph Seymour," 1056.
105. Synan, "The Azusa Street Revival: Celebrating 100 Years," 8. People were only allowed to enter the upper room for their Pentecostal Spirit baptism once they had first been saved and sanctified.
106. Unknown author, "At Azusa Mission," *The Apostolic Faith* 1:8 (312 Azusa Street, Los Angeles, CA: May, 1907), 2.
107. Robeck, Jr., "Azusa Street Revival," 349.
108. Bartleman, *How Pentecost Came to Los Angeles*, 54.
109. Unknown author, "Beginning of World Wide Revival," *The Apostolic Faith* 1:5 (312 Azusa Street, Los Angeles, CA: January, 1907), 1. "It is a continual upper room tarrying at Azusa Street. It is like a continual campmeeting or convention. All classes and nationalities meet on a common level. One who came for the first time said, 'The thing that impressed me the most was the humility of the people, and I went to my room and got down on my knees and asked God to give me humility.'"
110. Robeck Jr., *The Azusa Street Mission and Revival*, 14.
111. Louis Osterberg, "Filled with God's Glory," *The Apostolic Faith* 1:7 (312 Azusa Street, Los Angeles, CA: April, 1907), 4. "And before the meeting was over, I was fully satisfied and convinced that it was the mighty power of God that was working. From that time on I hungered more and more and felt that I could not be fully satisfied until the blessings of the Pentecostal life were mine."
112. Unknown author, "To the Baptised Saints," *The Apostolic Faith* 1:9 (312 Azusa Street, Los Angeles, CA: June to September, 1907), 2.
113. *The Apostolic Faith* 2:13 (312 Azusa Street, Los Angeles, CA: May, 1908), 3.
114. Unknown author, "Questions Answered," *The Apostolic Faith* 1:11 (312 Azusa Street, Los Angeles, CA: October-January, 1908), 2.

115. Bartleman, *How Pentecost Came to Los Angeles*, 59-60. "The meetings started themselves, spontaneously, in testimony, praise and worship... A dozen might be on their feet at one time, trembling under the mighty power of God. We did not have to get our cue from some leader... We were shut up to God in prayer in the meetings, our minds on Him. All obeyed God, in meekness and humility. In honor we 'preferred one another.' The Lord was liable to burst through any one. We prayed for this continually. Some one would finally get up anointed for the message. All seemed to recognize this and gave way. It might be a child, a woman, or a man. It might be from the back seat, or from the front. It made no difference. We rejoiced that God was working. No one wished to show himself. We thought only of obeying God. In fact there was an atmosphere of God there that forbade any one but a fool attempting to put himself forward without the real anointing. And such did not last long. The meetings were controlled by the Spirit, from the throne. Those were truly wonderful days. I often said that I would rather live six months at that time than fifty years of ordinary life."

116. Ibid., 58-59. "No subjects or sermons were announced ahead of time, and no special speakers for the hour. No one knew what might be coming, what God would do. All was spontaneous, ordered by the Spirit. We wanted to hear from God, through whomever He might speak. We had no 'respect of persons.' The rich and educated were the same as the poor and ignorant, and found a much harder death to die. We only recognized God. All were equal. No flesh might glory in His presence. He could not use the self-opinionated. Those were Holy Ghost meetings, led of the Lord. It had to start in poor surroundings, to keep out the selfish, human element. All came down in humility together, at His feet. They all looked alike, and had all things in common in that sense at least. The rafters were low, the tall must come down. By the time they got to 'Azusa' they were humbled, ready for the blessing. The fodder was thus placed for the lambs, not for giraffes. All could reach It."

117. Unknown author, "To the Baptised Saints," *The Apostolic Faith* 1:9 (312 Azusa Street, Los Angeles, CA: June to September, 1907), 2. "The Lord wants us to keep that fresh anointing, that sweet anointing that we had when the Holy Ghost first fell upon us."

118. Ibid.
119. See Jennifer A. Miskov, "Giving Room to the Anointing: Carrie Judd Montgomery's Impact on Women in Ministry" in *Global Pentecostal and Charismatic Studies series volume on Women in Leadership* by eds. Peg English de Alminana and Lois Olena (Leiden, Netherlands: Brill, 2016).
120. Bartleman, *How Pentecost Came to Los Angeles*, 59-60.
121. Unknown author, "The Old Time Pentecost," *The Apostolic Faith* 1:1 (312 Azusa Street, Los Angeles, CA: September 1906), 1. "People are seeking at the altar three times a day and it is hard to close at night on account of seekers and those who are under the power of God."
122. Bartleman, *How Pentecost Came to Los Angeles*, 58-59.
123. Ibid., 102. "And He did not disappoint us. One sister sang and spoke in 'tongues' for five full hours. Souls were saved. The saints were wonderfully built up and strengthened by the presence of the Lord. A number received the 'baptism,' and the mission became full fledged for 'Pentecost.' One Sunday night the hall was packed out, to the middle of the street. I went to the hall one morning to look up the folks, who had not come home. Several had stayed all night. I found them lost to all but God. They could not get away. A very shekinah glory filled the place. It was awesome, but glorious."
124. Ibid., 62. "Someone might be speaking. Suddenly the Spirit would fall upon the congregation. God himself would give the altar call. Men would fall all over the house, like the slain in battle, or rush for the altar en masse, to seek God. The scene often resembled a forest of fallen trees. Such a scene cannot be imitated. I never saw an altar call given in those early days. God himself would call them. And the preacher knew when to quit. When He spoke we all obeyed. It seemed a fearful thing to hinder or grieve the Spirit. The whole place was steeped in prayer. God was in His holy temple. It was for man to keep silent."
125. Ibid., 53.
126. *The Apostolic Faith* 1:4 (312 Azusa Street, Los Angeles, CA: December, 1906), 1. "The great Shekina glory is still resting upon us as a pillar of fire by night and a pillar of cloud by day, where hundreds and thousands of souls have come and been blest through the mighty power of our blessed Lord. Hungry and thirsty souls are

coming from hundreds and thousands of miles to get their personal Pentecost, and receiving and taking the glad tidings back home to hungry and thirsty souls that are waiting their arrival."

127. Unknown author, "Beginning of World Wide Revival," *The Apostolic Faith* 1:5 (312 Azusa Street, Los Angeles, CA: January, 1907), 1.

128. Unknown author, "Everywhere Preaching the Word," *The Apostolic Faith* 1:10 (312 Azusa Street, Los Angeles, CA: September, 1907), 1. At a camp meeting in the dining tent it was said, "We enjoyed some blessed times in the Spirit there, and also in the workers' dining tent, before we got the big tabernacle on the 'all things common' line. One morning while at prayer after breakfast, the power of God so came on us that ten of the workers were slain and we did not get away till noon. We had a foretaste of heaven."

129. Bartleman, *How Pentecost Came to Los Angeles*, 64.

130. Ibid., 83. "Sunday, September 9 [1906], was a wonderful day. Several were stretched out under the power for hours. The altar was full all day, with scarcely any cessation to the services. Several received the 'baptism.' In those days we preached but little. The people were taken up with God. Brother Pendleton and myself could generally be found lying full length on the low platform on our faces, in prayer, during the services. It was almost impossible to stay off our faces in those days. The presence of the Lord was so real. And this condition lasted for a long time. We had but little to do with guiding the meetings. Everyone was looking to God alone. We felt almost like apologizing when we had to claim any attention from the people, for announcements. It was a continuous sweep of victory. God had their attention. The audience would be at times convulsed with penitence. God dealt deeply with sin in those days. It could not remain in the camp."

131. Unknown author, "At Azusa Mission," *The Apostolic Faith* 1:8 (312 Azusa Street, Los Angeles, CA: May, 1907), 2. "In Azusa Mission, there is a prayer room upstairs for the sick. People get healed there every day." See also unknown author, "Healing," *The Apostolic Faith* 1:6 (312 Azusa Street, Los Angeles, CA: February-March, 1907), 6: "On the 18th of this month, there was a woman healed in the upper room of the Azusa Street Mission that was paralyzed in her whole right side. She could not move her hand or her foot. But in five or ten minutes after prayers were offered for her, we asked her to rise

and walk, and the power of God went through her and she arose and walked. Now she can walk just as well as ever and use her hand. Praise God! Hallelujah!" And *The Apostolic Faith* 1:1 (312 Azusa Street, Los Angeles, CA: September, 1906), 3: "A sister was healed of consumption when she had but a part of a lung left. She lay in a trance for three days and saw heaven and hell and unutterable things. She received the Pentecost and gift of tongues and feels called to a foreign land."

132. *The Apostolic Faith* 1:1 (312 Azusa Street, Los Angeles, CA: September, 1906), 3.

133. Unknown author, "Beginning of World Wide Revival," *The Apostolic Faith* 1:5 (312 Azusa Street, Los Angeles, CA: January, 1907), 1.

134. Bartleman, *How Pentecost Came to Los Angeles*, 57-58.

8. SEYMOUR'S LIFE AFTER THE REVIVAL

135. Seymour cited Isaiah more than any other book in his preaching. This was in line with how many others in the African-American tradition also preached. See Robeck, Jr., "William Joseph Seymour," 1053-1058.

136. Robeck, Jr., "William Joseph Seymour," 1053-1058.

137. *The Apostolic Faith* 2:13 (312 Azusa Street, Los Angeles, CA: May, 1908), 1. Many once referred to the Azusa Mission as the blessed old "Manger Home" because it was the birthplace for many nations receiving the Pentecostal blessing.

138. Synan and Fox, Jr., *William J. Seymour: Pioneer of the Azusa Street Revival*, 117.

139. Vinson Synan, "The Lasting Legacies of the Azusa Street Revival," *Enrichment Journal* (Springfield, MO: The General Council of the Assemblies of God, 2016), accessed January 30, 2016 http://enrichmentjournal.ag.org/200602/200602_142_Legacies.cfm. Some of those indirectly impacted by Azusa "included Thomas Ball Barratt (Western Europe and Great Britain), Daniel Berg and Gunnar Vingren (Brazil), Luigi Francescon (Italy, Argentina, and Brazil), and Ivan Voronaev (Russia and the Slavic nations)."

140. Martin, *The Life and Ministry of William J. Seymour*, 233.

141. Roberts Liardon, *God's Generals: Why They Succeeded and Why Some*

Failed (New Kensington, PA: Whitaker House, 1996), 163.

142. Gina A. Bellofatto and Todd M. Johnson, "Key Findings of Christianity in Its Global Context, 1970-2020," *International Bulletin of Missionary Research* 37.3 (2013), 157-164. They also believe that there will be over seven million Pentecostals and charismatics by 2020. See also Robert Crosby, "A Pentecostal Growth Explosion – Over A-Fourth of Christendom," May 24, 2012, http://www.patheos.com/blogs/robertcrosby/2012/05/a-pentecostal-growth-explosion-over-a-fourth-of-christendom/. (accessed January 25, 2016). "The Pentecostal movement itself continues to grow at a rapid rate. It is arguably the fastest-growing component of Christendom today. Johnson, Director of the Center for the Study of Global Christianity (located at Gordon-Conwell Theological Seminary) gave a new report on the status of Spirit-Empowered churches. The Center has recently adopted the term "Renewalists" to represent the three key sectors of this movement, including Classical Pentecostals, Main-line Denominational Charismatics and Independent Charismatics. At present, it is estimated that these groups combined make up 584 million worldwide, or 26 percent of all Christians."

143. Synan, "The Azusa Street Revival: Celebrating 100 Years," 6. "From this single revival has issued a movement which a century later numbers over one half billion persons from almost every nation of the world. In addition to these Pentecostals, there are millions of charismatics and neocharismatics in every denomination who can trace at least part of their spiritual heritage to the Azusa Street meeting...Indeed, with the turn of the 21st century, the Pentecostals and charismatics are second only to the Roman Catholic Church in the number of adherents. Also as the church has entered the new century, Pentecostals continue to be the fastest growing family of Christians in the world."

144. While the specific origins of Pentecostalism are still highly controversial, most scholars can at least admit that great significance was added to the movement as a whole through what happened at the Azusa Street Revival. See Anderson, *Spreading Fires*, 48.

9. PREPARING TO STEWARD
THE NEXT AWAKENING

145. Much of this section is influenced by Miskov, "Coloring Outside the Lines," 94–117.

146. See Jennifer A. Miskov, "There's a Tidal Wave of Revival on the Horizon," *Charisma Magazine* online (February 17, 2014), http://www.charismamag.com/spirit/revival/19794-there-s-a-tidal-wave-of-revival-on-the-horizon

147. Norman Grubb, *Rees Howells Intercessor* (Fort Washington, PA: Christian Literature Crusade, 1952), 29-30. "Under the influence of the Spirit there was an irresistible power."

148. Unknown author, "Beginning of World Wide Revival," *The Apostolic Faith* 1:5 (312 Azusa Street, Los Angeles, CA: January, 1907), 1. "From the little mustard seed faith that was given to a little company of people waiting on God in a cottage prayer meeting, a great tree has grown, so that people from all parts of the country are coming like birds to lodge in the branches thereof. (Matt. 13:31-32.) The faith is still growing, and we are still just in the beginning, earnestly contending for the faith once delivered unto the saints."

12. THE OPPORTUNITY OF
A LIFETIME IS AT OUR DOOR

149. Bartleman, *How Pentecost Came to Los Angeles*, 65.

150. Stanley Howard Frodsham, *Smith Wigglesworth: Apostle of Faith* (London: Elim Publishing Co., Ltd, 1949), 82. Smith Wigglesworth once said, "Fear looks; faith jumps."

151. This section is heavily influenced by the allegory based on Joshua and Caleb's journey by Jennifer A. Miskov, *Silver to Gold: A Journey of Young Revolutionaries* (Birmingham, UK: Silver to Gold, 2009).

14. A NEW JESUS REVOLUTION

152. *The Apostolic Faith* 1:11 (312 Azusa Street, Los Angeles, CA: October-January, 1908), 4. "Not seeking to get some great thing more than somebody else. The Lord God wants you just as humble

as a baby, looking for Him to fill you with more of God and power. If you get your eyes on manifestations and signs you are liable to get a counterfeit, but what you want to seek is more holiness, more of God."

153. Rolland Baker, *Keeping the Fire: Sustaining Revival Through Love: The Five Core Values of Iris Global* (Kent, UK: River Publishing 2015), 141-142. Heidi Baker's husband Rolland, who has also seen the deaf hear, the blind see, the dead raised, and is a powerful voice for our generation in his own right, says that after all is said and done, knowing Jesus is still what matters most. In his *Keeping the Fire*, he talks about how "Iris is not about us. It is about *Jesus*. Revival is not about manifestations or miracles; it is about the Reviver, Jesus our Savior. We only have one destination, one home, one reality, one resting place, one source, one motivation, one reward, one possession, one point of contact with God, one source of real satisfaction – and that is Jesus. We cannot overemphasize Him in any way. He is all we have and everything we need. Love is a gift of relationship, not just self-sacrifice. The secret place is not necessarily found in a prayer closet or a posture of soaking, or in battling for a just cause, or in a massive prayer and fasting effort. Even the most amazing miracles can leave us lonely and without relationship. We can run out of motivation advancing the noblest ideals and working at all levels to transform society. We can minister until we have no more strength, and still go home and lie in bed without the relationship for which our hearts are made. Everything is okay with relationship. It is all that Jesus cares about, all that motivates Him. He could do many more amazing miracles and dazzle the world with His powers, but He is interested only in relationship."

RESOURCES BY JENNIFER A. MISKOV

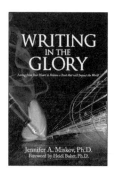

BOOKS

Writing in the Glory: Living from your Heart to Release a Book that will Impact the World. Redding, CA: Silver to Gold, 2015.

Life on Wings: The Forgotten Life and Theology of Carrie Judd Montgomery. Cleveland, TN: CPT Press, 2012.

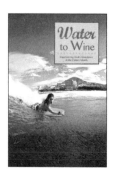

Water to Wine: Experiencing God's Abundance in the Canary Islands. Anaheim, CA: Silver to Gold, 2011.

Spirit Flood: Rebirth of Spirit Baptism for the 21st Century (In Light of the Azusa Street Revival and the Life of Carrie Judd Montgomery). Birmingham, UK: Silver to Gold, 2010.

Silver to Gold: A Journey of Young Revolutionaries. Birmingham, UK: Silver to Gold, 2009.

BOOKS WITH OTHER AUTHORS

- *Defining Moments.* Bill Johnson with Jennifer A. Miskov. New Kensington, PA: Whitaker House, 2016.

CHAPTERS IN BOOKS

- "The Liturgy of the Welsh Revival and the Azusa Street Revival: Connections, Similarities and Development" in *Scripting Pentecost* by editors A.J. Swaboda and Mark Cartledge. London, UK: Ashgate, 2016.

- "Giving Room to the Anointing: Carrie Judd Montgomery's Impact on Women in Ministry" in *Global Pentecostal and Charismatic Studies series volume on Women in Leadership* by editors Peg English de Alminana and Lois Olena. Leiden, Netherlands: Brill, 2016.

ACADEMIC JOURNAL ARTICLES

- "Missing Links: Phoebe Palmer, Carrie Judd Montgomery, and Holiness Roots within Pentecostalism," in *PentecoStudies: An Interdisciplinary Journal for Research on the Pentecostal and Charismatic Movements* 10:1 (2011).

- "Coloring Outside the Lines: Pentecostal Parallels with Expressionism. The Work of the Spirit in Place, Time, and Secular Society?" *Journal of Pentecostal Theology 19 (2010) 94–117.*

MAGAZINE ARTICLES

- "The Call Azusa: The Opportunity of a Lifetime Knocks at Our Door" in *Charisma Magazine Online* 2/17/2016

- "Baptism of Fire: Preparing for the Next Azusa Street Revival," in *Charisma Magazine Online* 1/28/2016

- "Heidi Baker, Todd White Watch Holy Spirit Fall on Thousands" in *Charisma News* 7/14/2015

- "Spirit Break Out: Unexpectedly Encountering God at an Academic Conference" in *Ministry Today Online* 3/19/2014

- "There's a Tidal Wave of Revival on the Horizon" in *Charisma Magazine Online* 2/17/2014

- "Carrie Judd Montgomery: A Passion for Healing and the Fullness of the Spirit" in *Assemblies of God Heritage Magazine*, 2012

- "The Power of the Healing Testimony" in *Pentecostal Evangel* September 2014

- "Kindred Spirits," *Alliance Life*, March 2011

- "Healing on the Streets," *Youthwork Magazine* (UK)

A FEW ARTICLES FROM JEN'S BLOG

- "Tapping into the Power of the Testimony: Launching into Greater Destiny"

- "Feasting on God: The Lost Art of Fasting"

- "Step into the Impossible: Miracle Flight to England"

- "God Holds the Key to Our Destiny"

- "How Halloween is a Catalytic Day for Reformation, the Welsh Revival, and Destiny"

You can access Jen's books and other writings at
silvertogold.com

ABOUT THE AUTHORS

Jennifer A. Miskov is the founding director of Destiny House, a ministry that cultivates communities of worshippers who do life together in God's presence and who launch people into their destinies from a place of intimacy with God and connection with family. At Destiny House, they have a one hundred year vision for worship to be released in the context of family. Jen also teaches revival history classes at Bethel School of Supernatural Ministry as well as facilitates Writing in the Glory workshops in various places. Jen is ordained by Heidi Baker with Iris Global and also by Bill Johnson with Bethel Church of Redding, California. Jen loves to lead people into life changing encounters with Jesus through her writing, teaching, and ministry. She also has a Ph.D. in Global Pentecostal and Charismatic Studies from the University of Birmingham, U.K. *Learn more at silvertogold.com.*

Heidi Baker's greatest passion is to live in the manifest presence of God and to carry His glory, presence, and love. She longs to see many others lay their lives down for the sake of the Gospel and come home to the Father's love. Rolland and Heidi Baker founded Iris Ministries, now Iris Global, in 1980. In 1995, they were called to the poorest country in the world at the time, Mozambique, and faced an extreme test of the Gospel. They began by pouring out their lives among abandoned street children. As the Holy Spirit moved miraculously, a revival movement was birthed. The move of God has spread throughout the bush all across Mozambique's ten provinces, and to the neighboring nations.

Heidi is now "Mama Aida" to thousands of children, and oversees a broad holistic ministry that includes Bible schools, a mission school, medical clinics, church-based orphan care, well drilling, primary and secondary schools, vocational schools, cottage industries, widow's programs, and healing outreaches in remote villages. Iris Global has planted over ten thousand Partners in Harvest churches, and now has bases in 36 nations. Heidi earned her B.A. and M.A. degrees from Southern California College (now called Vanguard University) and her Ph.D. from King's College, University of London. *Learn more at irisglobal.org.*

Lou Engle is both an intercessor for revival and visionary co-founder of TheCall, a prayer-and-fasting movement responsible for gathering hundreds of thousands around the globe. Lou's life and teachings have inspired countless intercessors to pray more effectively. He has helped establish key houses of prayer and justice movements that daily contend for spiritual breakthrough in America and abroad, including the pro-life prayer ministry, Bound 4 Life. Presently, Lou resides in Pasadena, California with his incredible wife, Therese, and is deeply proud of his seven children. *Learn more at thecall.com.*

Bill Johnson and his wife Beni are the Senior Pastors of Bethel Church in Redding, California. Bill is a fifth generation pastor with a rich heritage in the things of the Spirit. Together they serve a growing number of churches that have partnered for revival. This apostolic network has crossed denominational lines in building relationships that enable church leaders to walk in both purity and power. Bill teaches that we owe the world an encounter with God, and that a Gospel without power is not the Gospel that Jesus preached. *Learn more at Bjm.org.*